Bridge
Basics

Other books by Ron Klinger
published by Houghton Mifflin Company

Guide to Better Bridge
Guide to Better Card Play

By Hugh Kelsey and Ron Klinger

Instant Guide to Bridge

Standard American Edition

BRIDGE BASICS

RON KLINGER

A Master Bridge Series title
in conjunction with Peter Crawley

Houghton Mifflin Company
Boston • 1991

To Suzie

For information about permission to reproduce selections from
this book, write to Permissions, Houghton Mifflin Company,
2 Park Street, Boston, Massachusetts 02108.

Library of Congress Cataloging-in-Publication Data

Klinger, Ron.
Bridge basics : an introduction to good bridge / Ron Klinger ;
introduction by Alan Truscott. — 4th ed., American standard ed.
p.   cm.
"A Master bridge series title."
ISBN 0-395-59106-6
1. Contract bridge.   I. Title.
GV1282.3.K62   1991   91-7368
795.41'5 — dc20   CIP

Printed in the United States of America

BP 10 9 8 7 6 5 4 3 2 1

CONTENTS

INTRODUCING RON KLINGER
by Alan Truscott

Look around the world of bridge in search of someone who is at the top of the tree as a player, teacher and writer and you will find perhaps half a dozen candidates. One of them, and only one, is outside North America, which is why he is not as well known as he ought to be.

His name is Ron Klinger, and his residence is in Sydney, Australia, long the home of some of the world's best players. I first met him two decades ago when I took an expert team for a Down-Under tour and encountered a young Professor of Law who was describing the play for large audiences with intelligence and wit.

Soon afterwards he abandoned academic pursuits, which may have been a loss to the Law but was certainly a gain for the bridge community. He rapidly turned himself into Australia's Mr. Bridge, the equivalent perhaps of Charles Goren in his heyday in the forties and fifties. However the parallel is inexact, for Goren had many collaborators and Klinger is a one-man band.

Like Goren, Klinger made his name to the bridge public by a string of impressive playing performances. He has lost count of the number of major titles he has won, and enumerating his international appearances is not much easier. Down-Under, as Up-Over, every expert wants to carry the flag in foreign parts and fierce selection battles occur annually.

He is almost always in the thick of it, and is the most successful player of his generation. His total international appearances may soon rival that of the legendary Tim Seres, who helped earlier Australian teams to challenge effectively at world level.

Specifically Klinger has played five times in the Far East Championships, winning the Teams in 1970 and the Pairs twice, in 1985 and 1987. On a wider scene he has played in six of the biennial Olympiads — the bridge misnomer for an Olympic — and at three consecutive ones, in 1976, 1978 and 1980, he won the Bols Brilliancy Prize: for the best-played hand in 1976, and for his bridge journalism on the other occasions. Since there are hundreds of candidates for this prize his string is not only remarkable but unique. In the Bermuda Bowl, in which the representation is by zones, the South Pacific is represented by Australia and New Zealand. In this event Klinger made his second appearance in 1989, in Perth, and the team reached the semifinal before losing to the American defending champions after a hard fight.

For occasions such as this Klinger has created his own 'Power' system, which is a clever blend of the old and the new. Most of the opening bids follow the recipe that Dr. Paul Stern devised for the Austrian team which won the first world championship, played in 1937. An updated version, 'New South Wales', was popular in Sydney with Seres and his group. Klinger has taken some elements and added hypermodern two-bids and relays, a mixture that he does not offer to his students and readers. It is reserved for his partners, who are required to have good memories.

In a 13-year stint as Editor, starting in 1972, Klinger made *Australian Bridge* one of the world's best bridge magazines. At the same time he began writing a series of successful books on the game. One of them, 100 WINNING BRIDGE TIPS, has proved very popular in the United States and as these lines are written, he is at work on a sequel. He personally published many of the original Australian editions of his books using an early desk-top publishing set-up.

He is, as I know from hearing him, a superb teacher, and regularly projects his knowledge of the game to large groups in various parts of his continent. Like all the best bridge instructors, he provides his students with prepared deals to illustrate the lesson. This involves not only careful planning but also laborious work, as I know from personal experience.

When a vivacious lady named Suzie became his bride in 1974 she immediately found that bridge would have a big impact on her life. The money in the kitty was just sufficient either to take a honeymoon or to publish his first book. (It proved a great success.) Suzie attends to all the administrative details that her husband's work entails. Their children, Ari and Keri, join in much of the family travel, and if they miss some schooling, the parents promptly turn themselves into substitute teachers.

I began by saying that Klinger is a top player, writer and teacher. But he is also a commentator, game director, editor, publisher, game inventor, group travel co-ordinator and tour guide. What else is there? Time will tell.

Alan Truscott
January 1991

INTRODUCTION TO THE BRIDGE BEGINNER

Bridge is fun to play, but the better you play, the more fun it is. As you improve, you will be fascinated at discovering how much there is to the game. Despite popular opinion to the contrary, bridge is not difficult to learn.

This book is the product of many classes given to beginners and improving players. It is intended for those who know nothing about bridge and also for those who already know how the game is played but who wish to learn Standard American bidding or to improve their game. The book can be used as a self-teacher or in conjunction with bridge classes.

If you are an absolute beginner, it would be worthwhile to play through the games for beginners set out in Appendix 1 : From Whist To Bridge. After you have become familiar with the mechanics of the game, proceed to Chapter 1.

For the reader who can already play, do not try to memorise everything as you go, but do pay close attention to the examples and the play hands in each chapter. It is worth re-reading the text every six months or so until you are confident you know the contents. It would be beneficial to test yourself on the exercises as you go. These exercises simulate countless ordinary bidding situations and by scoring well on the exercises, you will build up confidence and also score well at the table when the everyday problems occur.

This book is not for the expert and will not make you an expert bridge player. It does not deal with expert bidding, expert play or expert defense, but it does cover the ordinary, standard situations, *the basics* that make up 95% of the game and in which most ordinary players go wrong. If you follow the recommendations, you will eliminate fundamental flaws from your game and pass from a novice to a competent, confident bridge player.

To improve, you should try to play as often as possible, for the more you play the more quickly you will improve. It is all very well to take lessons and read books, but much of bridge competence is based on experience. The more often you encounter a basic situation, the more readily you will be able to deal with it in future.

Above all remember that *bridge is a game to be enjoyed.* It can and should be a lot of fun and that is how you should approach it. I hope you derive as much enjoyment and satisfaction from it as I have. Happy bridging.

Ron Klinger, 1991

INTRODUCTION TO THE BRIDGE TEACHER

In conducting regular courses for bridge players, you will encounter two distinct types of players in classes for beginners: those who have never played bridge before (and may not even have played cards before) and those who have played before, who might have learnt at home or socially but who either know very little about bidding strategy and system rules or have not played for quite some time and have forgotten most of what they have learnt. It is quite a task to cater for both groups within the one class. If you dwell at length on the basic concepts of a 'trick', 'trumps', 'lead' and so on, as needed for the absolute beginners, the more advanced players are wasting their time since they know this fundamental area. On the other hand, if you cater for the more advanced members of your class, you run the far greater risk of leaving the absolute beginners floundering, losing interest and perhaps giving up the game.

Bridge Basics is suitable for classes for the beginner to improver standard. It is based on Standard American bidding and can be used for courses for absolute beginners. When dealing with absolute beginners, it is desirable to base the first class or even the first two classes on 'From Whist To Bridge' (see Appendix 1), before proceeding with Chapter 1. This would be a kind of 'Pre-Bridge' course. It is even sensible to hold two such pre-bridge classes (for those who have never played) before commencing the course proper (when those who have played previously join in).

Bridge Basics commences with the basics of all standard systems, the high card point count valuation and hand patterns. Chapter 2 covers the one-level suit opening bids for 5-Card Majors, Better Minor. Chapter 3 deals with the 1 NT opening and the treatment of balanced hand patterns, but does not include the 2 NT and 3 NT openings or slam bidding. These appear in later chapters in order to reduce the content at the start of the course.

If you prefer to teach a different method for suit openings, you can still use *Bridge Basics*. The opening bids when a 5-card or longer suit is held is standard (open the longer suit, with 5-5, open the higher-ranking), regardless of which approach is adopted. The changes come only for the 4-3-3-3, 4-4-3-2 and 4-4-4-1 patterns. Simply instruct your students which suit should be opened with these patterns (they can even write these instructions on page 18). When it comes to doing the exercises on opening the bidding on page 19, you will need to provide the answers which apply to your methods.

The play hands, quizzes and the exercises comply with system requirements, no matter which method is chosen. Thus each teacher of Standard American methods can cover the approach used locally.

Weak responding hands (under 10 points) are covered in Chapter 4 followed by strong responding hands (10 points or more) in Chapter 5. This division should simplify matters for both the teacher and the student. When we respond to partner's opening, we do think in terms of 'weak hand' or 'strong hand' and this conceptual approach should be of considerable assistance to students. Bidding by a passed hand is covered in Chapter 6 and strong openings (2-openings plus 2NT and 3NT) are in Chapter 7. Slam Bidding has a chapter of its own (Chapter 8) and so do Pre-emptive Openings (Chapter 9). Each chapter has its own set of exercises, partnership bidding practice and play hands.

There are three chapters dealing with competitive bidding, one on overcalls, one on takeout doubles and one on penalty doubles. In the chapter on takeout doubles, the suit response at the cheapest level is 0-9 (counting distribution) and the jump-response is 10-12. The no-trump responses conform to these ranges : the 1NT response to a double is 6-9 and the jump to 2NT is 10-12. The advantages of these point ranges are firstly, the ranges coincide with the standard ranges for responding to an opening bid (0-5, 6-9, 10 or more) covered in the earlier chapters, and secondly, the ranges for the no-trump responses dovetail with the ranges for a suit response. Both of these features mean that the ranges will strike students as familiar and students will not have to learn one set of ranges for suit bidding and a different one for no-trump responses.

The use of the 5-3-1 short suit count for suit responses to a takeout double has the effect of making the recommended ranges as accurate as necessary. The 3-2-1 short suit count is suggested as helpful in valuing a hand in order to make a takeout double even if it is not used in determining when to open the bidding and when to pass.

The student practice areas (the exercises, the partnership bidding and the play hands) provide more material than you can usually manage within a lesson. Choose the exercises you feel are most useful but the more student participation the better. In particular, do not omit the four play hands. Students often find this the most valuable part of the class. Exercises which you have not been able to cover in class can be set as homework and corrected at the start of the next class.

Suggested Structure of Bridge Courses :

The content of a course for bridge players will vary according to the number of classes available and the standard of the players. The following are possible curricula but, of course, you may decide to construct your own curriculum.

Content of bridge courses (relevant chapters in *Bridge Basics* in brackets)

A. Absolute beginners
12-week course :
1. Whist To Bridge I (p. 88)
2. Whist To Bridge II (p. 88)
3. Basics & suit openings (1, 2)
4. 1NT opening (3)
5. Weak responding hands (4)
6. Strong responding hands (5)
7. Two-openings (7)
8. Slam bidding (8)
9. Pre-empts (9)
10. Overcalls (10)
11. Takeout doubles (11, 12)
12. Revision and play practice

10-week course :
1. Whist To Bridge I (p. 88)
2. Whist To Bridge II (p. 88)
3. Basics & suit openings (1, 2)
4. 1NT opening (3)
5. Weak responding hands (4)
6. Strong responding hands (5)
7. Two-openings (7)
8. Slam bidding (8)
9. Overcalls (10)
10. Takeout doubles (11, 12)

8-week course :
1. Whist To Bridge (p. 88)
2. Basics & suit openings (1, 2)
3. 1NT openings (3)
4. Weak responding hands (4)
5. Strong responding hands (5)
6. Two-openings (7)
7. Slam bidding (8)
8. Overcalls and doubles (10, 11)

B. Improvers
12-week course :
1. Basics & suit openings (1, 2)
2. 1NT opening (3)
3. Weak responding hands I (4)
4. Weak responding hands II (4)
5. Strong responding hands I (5)
6. Strong responding hands II (5, 6)
7. Two-openings (7)
8. Slam bidding (8)
9. Pre-empts (9)
10. Overcalls (10)
11. Takeout doubles (11, 12)
12. Revision and play practice

10-week course :
1. Basics & suit openings (1, 2)
2. 1NT opening (3)
3. Weak responding hands (4)
4. Strong responding hands (5, 6)
5. Two-openings (7)
6. Slam bidding (8)
7. Pre-empts (9)
8. Overcalls (10)
9. Takeout doubles (11, 12)
10. Revision and play practice

8-week course :
1. Opening bids (1, 2, 3)
2. Weak responding hands (4)
3. Strong responding hands (5, 6)
4. Two-openings (7)
5. Slam bidding (8)
6. Pre-empts (9)
7. Overcalls (10)
8. Takeout doubles (11, 12)

Each of our classes lasts about 2½ hours and the content of each class after the first follows this structure : Correct homework; introduce new material; exercises; partnership bidding hands; coffee break; play hands.

We do not spend too much time on the homework, but this allows stragglers to come to class without missing any new material. Students bring their *Bridge Basics* to each class for the partnership bidding and the play hands.

You are urged to include the four play hands in each class, because they are at least as important as the main part of the lesson. Students learn much more quickly by playing than by listening and it is also more enjoyable.

The hands are set so that each player is declarer once. Except for the hands on defensive play (Chapter 10), each contract can be made and the idea is to give the relatively new players confidence in their ability. After the cards have been sorted out, the students should be allowed to bid the hands themselves. After their bidding is finished, go over the bidding with the class and any traps or errors should be explained.

The final contract should be the one in the book, not some other contract the students might have reached. The opening lead is made and corrected if the wrong lead was chosen, together with an appropriate explanation. The students should be left to play the hands on their own, though some brief advice can be given (e.g. "You need to ruff a club in dummy."). Students should be encouraged to play the cards in duplicate fashion, so that the hand can be conveniently replayed, if necessary.

Some declarers will go down, some will make overtricks, some defenses will be atrocious. After the hand, spend just a little time explaining the main thrust of the hand, but the students can go over the hands at home.

At the end of the course, encourage your students to play as often as possible. If you can arrange supervised practice sessions in conjunction with the course, so much the better. The aim of *Bridge Basics* is to make the game easy and fun for the students and if you can do the same, you will find the teaching of bridge to be a simple, pleasant and rewarding pastime.

Ron Klinger, 1991

CHAPTER 1
THE BASICS OF
ALL STANDARD SYSTEMS

THE HIGH CARD POINT COUNT

All standard systems start hand valuation by counting the high card content of the hand on this scale :

$$
\begin{array}{ccc}
A & = & 4 \\
K & = & 3 \\
Q & = & 2 \\
J & = & 1 \\
\end{array}
$$

Other points may be added to the high card point total but all hand valuation starts with the 4-3-2-1 count. The first thing you will do after you have sorted your cards into suits is to count and total your high card points. Then you will move on to noting the shape of the hand and the number of cards in each suit.

HAND PATTERNS AND HAND SHAPES

Each bridge hand contains 13 cards. The pattern of a hand describes the length of each suit in the hand starting with the longest suit, followed by the next longest and ending with the shortest suit. For example, to say that a hand is a 5-4-2-2 means that it contains a 5-card suit, a 4-card suit and two doubletons, while a 6-3-3-1 pattern means that the hand has a 6-card suit, two 3-card suits and a singleton.

There are three hand shapes : balanced, semi-balanced and unbalanced. A balanced hand has a 4-3-3-3, 4-4-3-2 or 5-3-3-2 pattern. It contains no void, no singleton and at most one doubleton. A semi-balanced hand has a 5-4-2-2, 6-3-2-2 or 7-2-2-2 pattern. It contains no void, no singleton, but will have two or three doubletons (in contrast to the balanced shapes which contain either one doubleton or no doubleton). Unbalanced hands consist of all the other possible patterns which have this common feature : they must contain a void or a singleton. The following table is a summary :

HAND SHAPES		
BALANCED	SEMI-BALANCED	UNBALANCED
4-3-3-3 4-4-3-2 5-3-3-2 No void, no singleton, at most one doubleton	5-4-2-2 6-3-2-2 7-2-2-2 No void, no singleton, two or three doubletons	5-4-3-1 5-5-2-1 and all other shapes which include a void or a singleton

Balanced hands are best for no-trump contracts. Since there is no short suit, at most one doubleton, there is little prospect for trumping and you are bound to follow suit almost throughout the hand. Therefore, a trump contract holds little attraction. Your approach would be to suggest no-trumps early in the bidding.

Unbalanced hands are best for trump contracts. As you hold either a void or a singleton, there is ample opportunity for trumping. Your best approach is to suggest one or more trump suits, reverting to no-trumps only as a last resort.

Semi-balanced hands are reasonable both for trump contracts and for no-trumps. There are two or three doubletons, making trumping attractive, while the absence of any singletons or voids makes no-trumps less risky.

1-SUITERS, 2-SUITERS AND 3-SUITERS

Hands are also described according to how many suits are available for bidding. For a suit to be biddable, it requires at least four cards. When a hand contains only one suit with four or more cards, it is called a one-suiter. When it contains two such suits, it is a two-suiter and with three such suits, it is termed a three-suiter. For example :

♠ 8 6 2	♠ A J 8 7 3	♠ A Q 7 6
♡ A 9 4	♡ K 4	♡ A K J 4
◊ A Q 9 8 3	◊ 8 2	◊ 9
♣ 5 4	♣ A Q J 9	♣ K Q J 3

This is a 10-point, balanced 1-suiter. Pattern : 5-3-3-2	A 15-point, semi-balanced 2-suiter. Pattern : 5-4-2-2	This is a 20-point, unbalanced 3-suiter. Pattern : 4-4-4-1

Exercise 1 : Hand shapes

Hands can be balanced, semi-balanced or unbalanced (see opposite).
What is the shape of each of these hands?

1.	♠ x x x x	2.	♠ x x x x x	3.	♠ x x x x	4.	♠ x x
	♡ x		♡ x		♡ x x		♡ x x x
	◇ x x x x		◇ x x		◇ x x		◇ x x x
	♣ x x x x		♣ x x x x x		♣ x x x x x		♣ x x x x x

5.	♠ x x x	6.	♠ x x x x	7.	♠ x x x	8.	♠ x x x x
	♡ x x x x		♡ x x x x		♡ x		♡ x x x x
	◇ x x x		◇ x x x		◇ x x x x		◇ x x x x
	♣ x x x		♣ x x		♣ x x x x x		♣ x

Exercise 2 : Points, shape and hand patterns

For each of the following hands, complete these details :

A. High Card Points   **B.** Shape   **C.** Pattern   **D.** 1-, 2- or 3-suiter

1.	♠ A 4	2.	♠ A K 4 2	3.	♠ A 9 3	4.	♠ K J 8 3 2
	♡ Q 8 6 3 2		♡ A 9 8 3		♡ Q 9 7 2		♡ A K J 4 3
	◇ K Q J 9		◇ K 8		◇ A Q 4		◇ 6
	♣ J 2		♣ 10 4 2		♣ Q 5 2		♣ J 8

A. ....

B. ....

C. ....

D. ....

5.	♠ K J	6.	♠ A K 9 4 2	7.	♠ A 10 7 2	8.	♠ 9 8 6 5 4 2
	♡ 7 5 3		♡ - - -		♡ 5		♡ A K 3
	◇ A J 9 8 4 2		◇ 6 5		◇ K J 10 9		◇ A Q 8 5
	♣ Q 6		♣ A J 8 7 4 3		♣ A Q 10 5		♣ - - -

A. ....

B. ....

C. ....

D. ....

POINTS NEEDED FOR GAMES AND SLAMS

IN ORDER TO MAKE	YOU + PARTNER NEED
3NT (9 TRICKS)	26 points
4♡ OR 4♠ (10 TRICKS)	26 points + 8 or more trumps
5♣ OR 5♢ (11 TRICKS)	29 points + 8 or more trumps
6-IN-A-SUIT (12 TRICKS)	33 points + 8 or more trumps
7-IN-A-SUIT (13 TRICKS)	37 points + 8 or more trumps

To say that 26 points or more are required to make a game in 3NT or that 33 points are needed before you should try for a small slam does not automatically guarantee that you will succeed if you have that number of points. However, the point requirements do mean that with the indicated number of points, you are more likely to succeed than fail. Nevertheless, skill in declarer play may still be required and even with skill, you may fail if the cards lie badly for your side. Bridge is not a game of guarantees and certainties. It is a game in which one takes calculated risks. The point requirements reveal when the risks are worth taking, when the odds of obtaining a significant score are in your favor.

If you and partner have enough strength to make a game but you fail to bid to a game, you have lost a valuable score. Similarly, if the partnership hands can produce a slam but slam is not bid, again a valuable score has been lost.

If the opposition bid and make a game, while you could have bid higher than their contract, even though you would have been defeated in your contract, you would have been better off to bid higher if the penalty for defeat would have been less than the value of their game. It is better to accept a small loss (a 'sacrifice') rather than let the opposition score a game or a slam.

You need not succeed in every game or every slam you bid. The rewards for finishing a rubber and the rewards for making a slam are so great that failing now and again is no tragedy and a failure rate in games or slams of about 1 in 4 is normal and expected. Suppose that you bid to 3NT four times and fail on two occasions but succeed on two occasions. Your success rate is only 50% but you are some 700 points in front because of the rubber bonus. The point to remember is that you need not be downhearted if you do not make every contract you bid.

TALKING BRIDGE

A little girl is watching her mother and three other ladies playing bridge. As the girl is taking a keen interest in the game, one of the ladies asks her, "And can you play bridge?" The girl replies, "No, but I can speak it."

Bridge players love to discuss bridge hands and there is an accepted method of description. If you wish to give a general account of the hand, state the number of high card points held and the hand pattern. For example:

♠ A J 8
♡ 7 3 2
◊ A K Q 9 5 3
♣ Q

A general description would be "I held a 16-point 6-3-3-1 hand..." A more precise description details the pattern by suit lengths in the rank order of the suits, spades, hearts, diamonds, clubs. Such a description of this hand would be "I held a 16-point 3-3-6-1..."

Most players, however, prefer to include the details of the actual high cards held. This is done by stating the honor cards in each suit, followed by the number of cards in that suit. Thus, A-9-6 is "ace third", K-Q-5-2 is "king-queen fourth" and A-K-J-8-4-2 is "ace-king-jack sixth". Other parts of the world use slightly different jargon, such as A-9-6 as "ace to three", K-Q-5-2 as "king-queen to four" and A-K-J-8-4-2 as "ace-king-jack to six". Where the suit contains no honor cards, the number of cards in the suit is followed by the word "rags". Thus, 8-6-2 would be "three rags" and 9-7-4-3-2 is "five rags".

If a doubleton is held, use "doubleton" rather than "second" for two specific cards (K-J would be "king-jack doubleton"), but where the suit has no honor card, use "two rags", "rag doubleton" or "doubleton rag". Where a singleton is held, the terminology is the honor card followed by "singleton" (such as "king singleton") or, with no honor, "singleton rag". It is also common to refer to a singleton honor as "bare" (such as "the bare king" or "king bare"). Slang for singleton is 'stiff', so that king-singleton becomes "stiff king" and a worthless singleton is simply "stiff".

The word "tight" is commonly used to mean "no more cards in the suit", so that king-singleton is "king tight", K-Q-doubleton is "king-queen-tight" and so on. Specific cards followed by a worthless card are denoted by the word "another" to mean "and one worthless card". Thus, K-3 becomes "king-another", A-Q-J-4 is "ace-queen-jack-another", and so on.

The hand near the top of the page could be described as "ace-jack third, three rags, ace-king-queen sixth and stiff queen."

BRIDGE NOTATION

When writing about bridge, it is conventional to write a bridge bid with the number first and the denomination second, just as though it were spoken. Thus, 1NT stands for One No-Trump, 3♠ stands for Three Spades, 4♡ is a bid of Four Hearts and so on. When writing about the cards held or played, the suit symbol is written first followed by the card(s), so that ♠7 stands for the seven of spades, ♡K stands for the king of hearts, and so on.

When writing a bidding sequence, a colon (:) separates the bids. Bids by your side are written without brackets and bids made by the opposing side are written inside brackets, for example, 1♠ : (2♣) : Pass : (3♣) ... When written bidding is in use, a diagonal stroke (/) indicates a pass, two diagonal strokes (//) = the final pass, double is X and redouble is XX.

STANDARD BIDDING SYSTEMS

A bidding system is just like a language — it is a means of communicating with your partner. However, the language of bridge allows only 15 legal words: one, two, three, four, five, six, seven, no-trumps, spades, hearts, diamonds, clubs, double, redouble and pass. Without any opposition bidding, there are only 35 bids available between 1 Club and 7 No-Trumps. With this restricted language, you try to describe to partner your thirteen cards, one of billions of possible hands.

Just as there are many languages, so there are many bidding systems. Just as some people are fluent in more than one language, so top players are adept at more than one system. Just as some languages are easier to learn than others, so some bidding systems are more efficient than others.

A bidding system is not really just one system. It consists of quite a number of sub-systems, each dependent on which opening bid is chosen. The requirements to open the bidding, which opening bid is to be chosen, the requirements to respond and what is meant by each possible response or rebid are stipulated by the system being learnt. Just as words can have different meanings in different languages, in different countries or in different ages, so bids frequently have different meanings in different systems.

Bridge Basics uses the most popular bidding system, Standard American. When you are just starting out at bridge, adopt one basic system, stick to it, learn it thoroughly and play it regularly for some two to three years. Once you have become proficient with your system and in general play, you may consider adopting some other system.

PART 1

STANDARD AMERICAN BIDDING

In this Part you will learn—

Which suit to start when you make a suit opening

When to open the bidding and when to pass

When to open with 1NT and when to prefer a suit opening

When to start with a 1-opening and when to prefer a 2-opening

How to respond to partner's opening—
when to choose a suit response, when to prefer a no-trump response and when to raise partner's suit; when to respond at the cheapest level and when to make a jump response; which suit to choose for your response when you have a choice of suits.

How to choose your rebids as opener or responder

How to judge when you should bid for game and when to stop lower; when to try for slam and when to be satisfied with game.

CHAPTER 2
OPENING WITH 1-IN-A-SUIT

When valuing for a suit opening, count high card points and add :

LENGTH POINTS :
1 point for each 5-card suit or 2 points for a 6-card or longer suit.

When Should You Open?

0-11 points: Do not open with a one-bid. With a long strong suit, your hand may be suitable for a pre-emptive opening of 3, 4 or 5 (see Chapter 9).

12 HCP : Open the bidding if your hand pattern is not 4-3-3-3.

12 total points but only 11 HCP or less (or 12 HCP with a 4-3-3-3 pattern) : Do not open with a 1-bid.

13-21 points: Open with 1-in-a-suit unless your hand fits a 1 NT opening. The 1-opening should contain at least 10 high card points.

22 points or more : Choose a 2-opening (see Chapter 7).

Which Suit Should You Open?

(1) Open your longest suit. Bid a 6-card minor ahead of a 5-card major.
(2) With two 5-card suits or two 6-card suits, open the higher-ranking.
(3) With no 5-card suit, open the longer minor.

● *Do not open 1♠ or 1♡ in first or second seat unless you have at least five cards in that suit.*

● *If you have 4-4 in the minors, open 1 ◇* (which is almost always a 4-card suit and so you should support diamonds with 4-card support).

● *If you have 3-3 in the minors, open 1♣.*

There is no minimum suit quality for an opening bid. The opening bid chosen depends solely on the length of the suits.

EXAMPLES

1. ♠ A J 9 4	2. ♠ A J 8	3. ♠ K J 9 6	4. ♠ J 8 4 3
♡ K Q	♡ K Q 9 6	♡ 7	♡ A Q 6
◇ Q J 7 4 3	◇ K 8 4 3	◇ Q 8 4 3	◇ A 9 8
♣ 7 2	♣ J 8	♣ A K 9 8	♣ K 6 2
Open 1◇.	Open 1◇.	Open 1◇.	Open 1♣.
Longest first.	Longer minor.	4-4 minors.	3-3 minors.

EXERCISE ON OPENING THE BIDDING

You are the dealer, neither side vulnerable. What action do you take?

1. ♠ A Q 7
   ♡ K Q 8 6
   ◇ 3
   ♣ J 8 7 4 2

2. ♠ A Q 7
   ♡ K Q 8 6 2
   ◇ 3
   ♣ J 8 7 4

3. ♠ A 8 7
   ♡ K Q 8 6 2
   ◇ 3
   ♣ J 8 7 4

4. ♠ A 8 7
   ♡ K Q 8 6 2
   ◇ 3
   ♣ A K Q 4

5. ♠ A K 7 6 3
   ♡ A 3
   ◇ 6
   ♣ K Q 9 5 2

6. ♠ Q 9 8 6 2
   ♡ A K J 7 3
   ◇ J 5
   ♣ 6

7. ♠ K Q J
   ♡ A 8 6 4 3
   ◇ K Q 7 4 2
   ♣ - - -

8. ♠ 8
   ♡ A J 9 7 2
   ◇ A Q J 8 4 3
   ♣ 6

9. ♠ A J 9
   ♡ K Q 7
   ◇ J 8 4 3
   ♣ J 7 2

10. ♠ A Q 9
    ♡ K Q 7
    ◇ J 8 4 3
    ♣ J 7 2

11. ♠ A K 9
    ♡ K J 7
    ◇ A 4 3
    ♣ K J 6 2

12. ♠ A Q 7 2
    ♡ A 9 8
    ◇ K 7 2
    ♣ 9 8 4

13. ♠ A Q 7 4
    ♡ J 8 7
    ◇ 6 2
    ♣ K Q 9 3

14. ♠ A K 8
    ♡ Q 9 6 2
    ◇ A 4
    ♣ 6 4 3 2

15. ♠ 6 2
    ♡ A J 8
    ◇ K 9 7 2
    ♣ A J 5 4

16. ♠ A K J 9
    ♡ A Q 3
    ◇ A 9 6 2
    ♣ Q 8

17. ♠ A Q 7 2
    ♡ K Q 9 3
    ◇ Q 7 6 2
    ♣ 4

18. ♠ A J 8 3
    ♡ Q 7 4 2
    ◇ 9
    ♣ A Q J 2

19. ♠ A K 3 2
    ♡ 7
    ◇ A Q 4 3
    ♣ A J 6 5

20. ♠ 9
    ♡ A 8 7 6
    ◇ K 9 4 3
    ♣ A Q 7 2

21. ♠ K 9 7 6 2
    ♡ A Q 3
    ◇ Q 7
    ♣ 8 6 5

22. ♠ A Q 9 7 6 2
    ♡ K Q 3
    ◇ 7 6 3
    ♣ 4

23. ♠ A J 8 7 4
    ♡ 4
    ◇ A Q 9 6 5
    ♣ 7 2

24. ♠ 8 7
    ♡ A J 8
    ◇ 6 4 2
    ♣ A K 6 4 3

25. ♠ K J 9 4
    ♡ A Q 8 5
    ◇ Q 7 4
    ♣ J 8

26. ♠ K J 9 4
    ♡ A Q 8 5
    ◇ Q 7
    ♣ J 8 6

27. ♠ K J 9
    ♡ 7 2
    ◇ Q 8 4 3
    ♣ A K 9 8

28. ♠ K J 9
    ♡ 8 7 6 2
    ◇ Q 8 3
    ♣ A K 9

PLAY HANDS OPENING WITH 1-IN-A-SUIT

Hand 1 : High-Cards-From-Shortage, Low-From-Length

Dealer North : Nil vulnerable

NORTH
♠ A Q J 7
♡ 9 4 3
♢ Q 7 5
♣ 6 4 2

WEST
♠ 6 5
♡ K Q J 10 8 2
♢ A 8
♣ J 8 5

EAST
♠ 10 9 4 3 2
♡ 5
♢ J 10 9 6
♣ K Q 10

SOUTH
♠ K 8
♡ A 7 6
♢ K 4 3 2
♣ A 9 7 3

WEST	NORTH	EAST	SOUTH
	Pass	Pass	1♢
1♡	1♠	Pass	1NT
Pass	Pass	Pass	

Lead : ♡ K. Top of sequence.

Correct play : After winning the ♡ A, play the ♠ K (high-from-shortage) followed by a spade to dummy and cash the other spade winners. Then lead a diamond to your king to set up a diamond trick. 7 tricks.

Wrong play : (1) Playing a low spade rather than the king first.
(2) Cashing the ♣ A before setting up a diamond trick. This would allow the defense to defeat the contract with hearts and clubs.

Hand 2 : Overcalling — The High-Card-From-Shortage Principle

Dealer East : Nil vulnerable

NORTH
♠ Q 10 9 2
♡ 3 2
♢ J 6
♣ 9 8 7 5 4

WEST
♠ 8 7 6
♡ K 6
♢ 9 4 3
♣ A K Q J 2

EAST
♠ A J 3
♡ Q 5 4
♢ A K 5 2
♣ 10 6 3

SOUTH
♠ K 5 4
♡ A J 10 9 8 7
♢ Q 10 8 7
♣ - - -

WEST	NORTH	EAST	SOUTH
		1♢	1♡
2♣	Pass	2NT	Pass
3NT	Pass	Pass	Pass

Lead : ♡ J. With an interior sequence (starting in the middle of a suit), lead top of where the sequence begins.

Correct play : Win the first heart and start on the clubs, playing the 10 from hand and the 2 from dummy (high-from-shortage). Cash the clubs, the A-K of diamonds and the ♠ A.

Wrong play : Failing to win with the ♣ 10 on the first or second round of clubs. This restricts you to only four club tricks, because of the unlucky 5-0 split and you could go off.

Hand 3 : Overtaking a winner in order to reach dummy

Dealer South: E-W vulnerable

NORTH
♠ 7 5 4 3
♡ Q J 10 9
◇ K J 10
♣ 10 6

WEST
♠ Q J
♡ 6 3 2
◇ Q 8 5 2
♣ A K Q J

EAST
♠ A K 10 2
♡ A 4
◇ 6 4 3
♣ 8 5 3 2

SOUTH
♠ 9 8 6
♡ K 8 7 5
◇ A 9 7
♣ 9 7 4

WEST	NORTH	EAST	SOUTH
			Pass
1◇	Pass	1♠	Pass
1NT	Pass	2NT	Pass
3NT	Pass	Pass	Pass

Lead: ♡ Q. Top of sequence. With equally long suits, lead the stronger.

Correct play: After winning the ♡ A, lead a low spade to the queen (high-from-shortage), followed by the ♠ J, overtaking with dummy's king or ace. Cash the spade winners and the clubs.

Wrong play: (1) Playing ♠ A or ♠ K on the first round of spades. (2) Failing to overtake the second round of spades with dummy's ace or king. This would leave two spade winners stranded in dummy.

Hand 4 : Overtaking a winner to gain access to dummy

Dealer West : Nil vulnerable

NORTH
♠ J 9 2
♡ A K 2
◇ K Q J
♣ 8 6 3 2

WEST
♠ A 6 4
♡ 10 9 8 5
◇ 8 4
♣ A 10 7 5

EAST
♠ 10 8 7 5 3
♡ Q 7 6
◇ 9 7 2
♣ K 9

SOUTH
♠ K Q
♡ J 4 3
◇ A 10 6 5 3
♣ Q J 4

WEST	NORTH	EAST	SOUTH
Pass	1♣	Pass	1◇
Pass	1NT	Pass	3NT
Pass	Pass	Pass	

Lead : ♠5, fourth-highest.

Correct play: West should win the ♠ A and return a spade. Lead a diamond to the king, cash the ◇ Q and then the ◇ J overtaking with dummy's ace. Cash the diamonds and then the hearts and the ♠ J. 9 tricks.

Wrong play: (1) Failing to overtake the third round of diamonds. This would allow the defense to beat 3NT. (2) Playing the ◇ A on the first or second round of diamonds. This will 'block' the diamonds and leave two diamond winners stranded in dummy.

CHAPTER 3
THE ONE NO-TRUMP OPENING

The 1 NT opening shows 16-18 points and balanced shape.

Most hands in the 13-21 zone start with a suit opening, but if your hand fits 1NT, prefer that opening to any other.

How To Handle Balanced Hands (4-3-3-3/4-4-3-2/5-3-3-2)

0-11 points : Pass

12 HCP : Open if 4-4-3-2 or 5-3-3-2. Pass in 1st or 2nd seat with a 4-3-3-3.

13-15 points : Open with 1-in-a-suit (see Chapter 2)

16-18 points : Open 1NT with any 4-3-3-3 or 4-4-3-2. Open 1NT with a 5-3-3-2 pattern if the 5-card suit is a minor. If a major, open 1♡ or 1♠.

19-21 points : Open with 1-in-a-suit (see Chapter 2)

22 points or more : See Chapter 7

WINNING STRATEGY :

When holding 26 points or more between you and partner, the partnership should bid a game.

Therefore, do not pass in the bidding until some game is reached if the partnership *could* have 26 points or more.

With 26 points together, game is a good chance.

With 25 points together, game is a fair chance.

With 24 points or less, game prospects are poor.

RESPONDING TO 1NT WITH A BALANCED HAND

0-7 points	:	PASS	Game prospects poor
8-9 points	:	2NT	Game possible, not sure
10-14 points	:	3NT	Good chances for game
15 points or more	:	See Chapter 8	Slam is possible
Unbalanced hands	:	See Chapter 4 and Chapter 5	

After 1NT : 2NT, opener should pass with 16 points (minimum) and continue to 3NT with 17-18 points (maximum). After 1NT : 3NT, opener must pass. After a 1NT, 2NT or 3NT opening, responder makes the decision how high to bid. Responder knows the combined strength, opener does not.

EXERCISES

A. What is your opening bid on these hands?

1.	♠ A Q 6	2.	♠ A Q 6	3.	♠ A Q 6 4 3	4.	♠ K J 6
	♡ K Q 8		♡ K Q		♡ K Q		♡ A Q 9
	◊ 7 6 5		◊ 7 6 5		◊ 7 6 5		◊ A 10 6 3
	♣ A J 9 4		♣ A J 9 4 2		♣ A J 9		♣ K Q 8

B. Partner opens 1NT. What is your response?

1.	♠ A 9 8	2.	♠ K 7 6	3.	♠ K 7 6	4.	♠ A K
	♡ K J 7		♡ 4 3		♡ 4 3		♡ 7 6 4
	◊ Q 9 8 4		◊ K 9 8 2		◊ K Q 8 2		◊ Q 9 8
	♣ 7 6 2		♣ 7 6 4 3		♣ 7 6 4 3		♣ K J 7 6 2

PARTNERSHIP BIDDING PRACTICE

West is the dealer on each hand. How should the bidding go?

WEST	EAST	WEST	EAST
1.	**1.**	**5.**	**5.**
♠ A J 7 2	♠ K Q 9	♠ 6 2	♠ A Q 7
♡ 7 6 4 3	♡ A 8	♡ Q 10 6	♡ K J 8 2
◊ 7 5	◊ A K 8 4	◊ K Q J 4	◊ A 7 6
♣ 8 7 2	♣ Q 9 4 3	♣ 8 7 4 3	♣ K 9 5
2.	**2.**	**6.**	**6.**
♠ K Q 8 6	♠ A 3 2	♠ A 3 2	♠ Q 6 4
♡ A 9	♡ 10 8 6	♡ A 10 9 2	♡ 8 3
◊ A K 4	◊ 9 6 3 2	◊ K Q 7 2	◊ J 10 5
♣ 9 7 6 2	♣ A 10 5	♣ K J	♣ Q 8 6 4 3
3.	**3.**	**7.**	**7.**
♠ A J 4	♠ K Q 3 2	♠ A 3 2	♠ Q J 6 5
♡ 8 3	♡ A 2	♡ 9 8 7	♡ A 6 2
◊ J 10 6	◊ 8 7 4 3	◊ A Q 4	◊ 8 3 2
♣ K 9 7 6 2	♣ A Q J	♣ A K 6 5	♣ 9 4 3
4.	**4.**	**8.**	**8.**
♠ A J 9 2	♠ K Q 7	♠ A 10 8	♠ K 7 5
♡ K Q J	♡ 8 4 2	♡ 9 2	♡ A 6 5 4
◊ K 9 2	◊ A 6 5 3	◊ A 10 8 6 4	◊ K Q 9 3
♣ Q 8 4	♣ 7 5 3	♣ Q 8 7	♣ A 5

PLAY HANDS FOR THE ONE NO-TRUMP OPENING

Hand 5 : High-Cards-From-Shortage, Low-From-Length

Dealer North : Nil vulnerable

WEST	NORTH	EAST	SOUTH
	Pass	Pass	1NT
Pass	Pass	Pass	

NORTH
♠ A Q 5 3
♡ 8 6 3
◇ 7 4 2
♣ 10 8 5

WEST
♠ 7 6
♡ J 10 9
◇ 10 6 3
♣ A Q 9 7 4

EAST
♠ 10 9 8 2
♡ Q 5 4
◇ K Q J 9
♣ K 2

SOUTH
♠ K J 4
♡ A K 7 2
◇ A 8 5
♣ J 6 3

Lead: ♣7. Against no-trumps, lead your long suit. Choose the fourth-highest when no sequence of three or more cards is held.

Play: East plays the ♣ K (3rd-hand-high), winning the trick, and returns a club. Return partner's lead unless you have a good alternative. The defenders win the first five tricks, South discarding red suit losers from both hands. Do not discard a spade. South wins the ♡ J switch at trick 6 and cashes four spades : king first, then jack, then low to dummy.

Hand 6 : The High-Card-From-Shortage Principle

Dealer East : Nil vulnerable

WEST	NORTH	EAST	SOUTH
		1NT	Pass
3NT	Pass	Pass	Pass

NORTH
♠ K 10 9 7 4
♡ 10
◇ 10 5 2
♣ 10 8 4 3

WEST
♠ Q J 2
♡ 8 6 5
◇ 7 6 4
♣ A K J 6

EAST
♠ 8 5 3
♡ A 4 3 2
◇ A K Q J
♣ Q 5

SOUTH
♠ A 6
♡ K Q J 9 7
◇ 9 8 3
♣ 9 7 2

Lead : ♡ K, top of the sequence.

Correct play: Win the ♡ A, play the *queen of clubs* (high-card-from-shortage first), then the other clubs and the four diamonds. 3NT made.

Wrong play: (1) Playing the ♣5 to dummy's ace and next cashing the ♣ K. This costs you the ♣ Q and you will fail by one trick.

(2) Playing the ♣5 to a winner in dummy and the 6 of clubs to your queen. This leaves two club winners in dummy and no entry to reach them.

Hand 7 : Overtaking a winner in order to reach dummy

Dealer South : E-W vulnerable

```
              NORTH
              ♠ Q 9 8
              ♡ 7 6 5 4
              ◇ A Q
              ♣ A K Q J
WEST                      EAST
♠ A 10 5 2               ♠ K J 3
♡ 10 3 2                 ♡ K Q J 9
◇ 9 6 3                  ◇ 8 7 5 2
♣ 9 7 5                  ♣ 10 6
              SOUTH
              ♠ 7 6 4
              ♡ A 8
              ◇ K J 10 4
              ♣ 8 4 3 2
```

WEST	NORTH	EAST	SOUTH
			Pass
Pass	1NT	Pass	2NT
Pass	3NT	All pass	

Lead: ♡ K. With equally long suits, lead the stronger. Top from sequence.

Correct play: After winning the ♡ A, lead a low diamond to the *ace* (high-from-shortage, low-from-length) and play ◇ Q, overtaking with dummy's king. Cash the diamond winners, followed by the clubs. 9 tricks.

Wrong play: (1) Winning the first round of diamonds with the queen. This 'blocks' the diamonds.
(2) Winning the first round of diamonds with the ace, but failing to overtake the ◇ Q with dummy's king.

Hand 8 : Overtaking a winner to gain access to dummy

Dealer West : Both vulnerable

```
              NORTH
              ♠ 8 7 4
              ♡ Q 9 6
              ◇ Q 8
              ♣ K J 9 4 2
WEST                      EAST
♠ A K J                  ♠ Q 10 3 2
♡ A 7 3                  ♡ 8 5 4
◇ A 5 4 2                ◇ 9 6 3
♣ 10 8 7                 ♣ A 6 5
              SOUTH
              ♠ 9 6 5
              ♡ K J 10 2
              ◇ K J 10 7
              ♣ Q 3
```

WEST	NORTH	EAST	SOUTH
1NT	Pass	Pass	Pass

Lead : ♣4, fourth-highest.

Correct play: If a low card is played from dummy, South plays the ♣ Q (third-hand-high) and returns a club. After winning the ♣ A, declarer should play a spade to the ace (high-from-shortage), cash the ♠ K (high-from-shortage) and lead the ♠ J, overtaking with dummy's queen to cash the ♠ 10 next. 7 tricks.

Wrong play: (1) Playing the ♠ J on the first or second round of spades, thus blocking the spade suit.
(2) Failing to overtake the ♠ J with dummy's queen on the third round of spades. The ♠ Q is now stranded.

CHAPTER 4
RESPONDING WITH WEAK HANDS

RESPONDING TO AN OPENING OF 1♣, 1◊, 1♡ OR 1♠

0-5 points : Pass

6-9 points : Bid, but only at the 1-level, *or* raise opener's suit to the 2-level

As an average hand contains 10 points, hands below that strength are considered weak. However, game is still possible when partner starts with a 1-opening in a suit, as partner can have 20 points or even a bit more. Therefore, **you should always respond to a suit bid with 6 points up,** but you would normally pass with a hand in the 0-5 point range.

When you are responding with a weak hand, it is important to keep the bidding at a low level initially, since partner may have only a minimum opening of about 13 points and then the partnership will have only 20 points together or a little more. With the strength evenly divided between your side and their side, it will be tough for you to make more than 7 or 8 tricks. Consequently, you may raise opener's suit to the 2-level with a weak hand, but otherwise you *must* remain at the 1-level. *You are not entitled to bid a new suit at the 2-level with 6-9 points, only with 10 points or more.*

Your Choice of Response : Raise Opener *or* New Suit *or* 1NT

Raise opener to the 2-level : 6-9 points + support for opener's suit.

A decent trump holding for your partnership is 8 trumps or more. With fewer than 8 trumps, the opponents will have almost as many as you or more than you, making your task to win very difficult. Since the partnership should have at least 8 trumps, you should have three trumps (or more) to support a 5-card suit (e.g. an opening bid of 1♡ or 1♠), four trumps (or more) to support a 4-card suit (e.g. a 1◊ opening), and five trumps (or more) to support a 1♣ opening, a suit that might be just a 3-carder.

When you do have support for partner, value your hand by counting the high card points and adding on points for the short suits where you might win tricks by ruffing. The short suit count when supporting is the **5-3-1** count : **5 for a void, 3 for a singleton, 1 for each doubleton.**

With 10 HCP and a 4-3-3-3 pattern with support for opener, a raise to the 2-level is acceptable. With less than 10 HCP but a total of 10 points after adding distribution, a raise to the 2-level is also acceptable.

Bid Your Own Suit (but only at the 1-level) : 6 points or more.

The suit you bid must contain at least four cards but it need not have any high cards in the suit itself. In other words, any 4-card suit is biddable for responder. A significant difference between bidding your own suit at the 1-level and raising opener to the 2-level or responding 1NT is that the raise is 6-9 and the 1NT response is 6-9, but the new suit response is 6 points *or more*. In other words, a new suit at the 1-level might be based on a strong hand, which you will reveal later in the bidding, but it need not have more than the minimum of 6 points. Because the raise to the 2-level is limited (6-9) and the 1NT response is limited (6-9), opener may pass these responses, but since the new suit response is unlimited (6 points *or more*), opener is obliged to rebid after a new suit response.

Where you have a choice of suits as responder, the order of preference is:

● Bid your longest suit first.

● With two 5-card suits or two 6-card suits, bid the higher-ranking.

● With two or three 4-card suits, bid the cheapest suit first.

'Cheapest' means the first available bid over partner's opening, not necessarily the lowest-ranking suit. If partner opened 1♡ and you have 4 spades and 4 clubs, 1♠ is a cheaper bid than 2♣. Likewise, if partner opened 1◇ and you hold 4 spades and 4 hearts, the cheaper suit is hearts and your response should be 1♡. This method of bidding your cheapest 4-card suit is called bidding your suits 'up-the-line'. Note that 'up-the-line' applies only to 4-card suits, *not to 5-card suits.*

The above order of preference in bidding suits is subject to the over-riding priority that *you are not permitted to bid a new suit at the 2-level unless you have at least 10 points.* Consequently, when you have only 6-9 points, you may occasionally be forced into bidding a suit which is not your normal first preference. Suppose partner opened 1◇ and you have 6 points with 4 spades and 5 clubs. You should respond 1♠. Your hand is not strong enough for 2♣.

Respond 1NT : 6-9 points, no support for opener, no suit at 1-level. If unable to raise opener and unable to bid a suit at the 1-level, respond 1NT as your last resort. Because of the importance of the rule requiring 10 points for a new suit at the 2-level, the 1NT response need not be balanced. If you have 10 HCP and a 4-3-3-3 pattern, prefer a 1NT response to a 2-level change of suit.

Resolving a Choice of Responses

What happens when your hand fits two or more responses? Perhaps you are able to support partner but you also have a suit of your own? Perhaps you could raise opener, bid your own suit or respond 1NT? The way to solve such conflicts will depend on whether your partner has opened with a major suit or with a minor suit. If you have only 6-9 points, this is the order of responding priorities :

If partner opened with a major suit :

1. Raise opener's major.

2. Bid 1♠ over 1♡ if unable to support hearts.

3. Respond 1NT.

If partner opened with a minor suit :

1. Change suit at the 1-level. Prefer a major to raising a minor.

2. Raise opener's minor.

3. Respond 1NT.

These priorities apply when responding with a weak hand. There may be different priorities when responding with a strong hand.

When changing suit in response to an opening bid of 1♣ or 1♢ , follow the normal rules when you have a choice of suits : longest suit first; the higher suit with two 5-card suits or two 6-card suits; up-the-line with 4-card suits.

EXERCISE

What is your response on these hands if partner opened . . .

(a) 1 Club?   (b) 1 Diamond?   (c) 1 Heart?   (d) 1 Spade?

1. ♠ J 4 3 2	2. ♠ K J 8 3	3. ♠ Q J 6 5 2	4. ♠ 9 8 4 2
♡ 8 6	♡ Q 5 4 2	♡ K 3	♡ 7 4
◇ A J 7 4 3	◇ 7 6	◇ 8 7 3	◇ A 8 5
♣ 9 5	♣ 8 7 3	♣ 9 4 2	♣ A 8 3 2
5. ♠ A Q 8 3	6. ♠ K 9 7 4 3	7. ♠ 4 3	8. ♠ 4 3
♡ 8 7 6 2	♡ 6	♡ A J 7 6	♡ Q 10 7 5 4
◇ 7 5	◇ A 7 6 5 4 2	◇ 6 2	◇ 9 8 6 4
♣ 4 3 2	♣ 4	♣ Q 10 7 5 4	♣ 3 2

EXERCISES ON RESPONDING WITH A WEAK HAND

A. Partner opens 1♣, next player passes. What is your response?

1.	♠ K J 8	2.	♠ K J 8	3.	♠ K J 8	4.	♠ K J 8 2
	♡ A 7 6		♡ A 7 6		♡ A 7 6 4		♡ A 7 6
	◇ 9 6 4		◇ 9 6 4 3		◇ 9 6 4		◇ 9 6 4
	♣ 8 7 3 2		♣ 8 7 3		♣ 8 7 3		♣ 8 7 3

5.	♠ A 7 4 2	6.	♠ A 7 4 2	7.	♠ A 7 4 2	8.	♠ 7 6
	♡ 7 6		♡ K 8 6 4		♡ 7 6		♡ K 8 6 4
	◇ K 8 6 4		◇ 7 6		◇ 9 4 3		◇ A 7 4 2
	♣ 9 4 3		♣ 9 4 3		♣ K 8 6 4		♣ 9 4 3

9.	♠ A 8 6 3 2	10.	♠ A 8 6 3 2	11.	♠ K J 7 5	12.	♠ K J 7 5
	♡ Q J 7 6 5		♡ 9		♡ J 8 4 3		♡ J 8 4 3
	◇ 9		◇ 7 2		◇ Q 9 8 3		◇ 2
	♣ 7 2		♣ Q J 7 6 5		♣ 2		♣ Q 9 8 3

13.	♠ A J 7 2	14.	♠ 7 6	15.	♠ Q 6	16.	♠ Q J 7 2
	♡ 7 6		♡ 5 4		♡ 5 4 2		♡ 6
	◇ 5 4		◇ A J 7 2		◇ A J 7		◇ A 9 7 6 4 3
	♣ Q 9 8 6 3		♣ Q 9 8 6 3		♣ 9 8 6 3 2		♣ 5 2

B. Partner opens 1♡, next player passes. What is your response?

1.	♠ K 7 6 4	2.	♠ 8 7 5 3	3.	♠ K 7	4.	♠ K 7 6
	♡ 8		♡ 8 2		♡ 6 2		♡ 2
	◇ Q 9 7 2		◇ A K 7		◇ Q 9 7 4		◇ Q 9 7 4
	♣ Q 8 4 3		♣ J 8 4 3		♣ Q 8 4 3 2		♣ Q 8 4 3 2

5.	♠ A 7	6.	♠ A J 7 2	7.	♠ A J 7 3 2	8.	♠ 7
	♡ J 7 6		♡ Q 9 8 3		♡ Q 8 7 5		♡ K 9 8 3
	◇ 9 8 7 4 2		◇ 7 6 4		◇ 9 4		◇ J 7 4 2
	♣ 8 4 3		♣ 4 2		♣ 6 2		♣ 8 6 4 2

Shut-out Jump-Raises

The jump raises to game in the major suits ($1\heartsuit$: $4\heartsuit$ and $1\spadesuit$: $4\spadesuit$) are used on weakish responding hands. They show about 6-9 high card points (could possibly be less), excellent trump support (more than the minimum needed for a raise) and unbalanced shape (must have a singleton or a void). The message is: "I have excellent support but am weak in high cards." They are called 'shut-out' because their function is to shut the next player out of the bidding. At the same time they serve as a warning to partner not to expect too much in high cards if partner has notions about a slam. They are also known as 'weak freaks' or 'gambling raises', but with the excellent support and unbalanced shape, it is not too much of a gamble.

Shut-out raises in the minor suits ($1\clubsuit$: $4\clubsuit$ *or* $1\clubsuit$: $5\clubsuit$ *or* $1\diamondsuit$: $4\diamondsuit$ *or* $1\diamondsuit$: $5\diamondsuit$) are available but are very rare since they bypass a possible 3NT contract. When used, however, they do show the same sort of hand as the shut-out raise in the major suits, namely weak in high cards (usually 6-9 high card points, occasionally even weaker), 5-card or longer trump support and an unbalanced hand (must contain a void or a singleton).

RESPONDING TO AN OPENING BID OF 1NT

Responding to 1NT with a balanced hand was covered in Chapter 3. Responding to 1NT with a weak unbalanced hand is different to responding to a suit opening, because the 1NT opening is closely defined, a balanced 16-18, while the suit opening has a wide range, 13-21 points and balanced, semi-balanced or unbalanced shape. You would pass a suit opening with 0-5 points but you are allowed, even encouraged, to respond to 1NT with a hopelessly weak hand, provided that you have a long suit:

1NT : 2-in-a-suit = 0-7 points and a 5-card or longer suit. Opener should pass this 2-level response but with 18 points and 4-card support, opener is permitted to raise responder's suit to the 3-level.

1NT : $2\clubsuit$ is commonly used as the Stayman Convention which you should certainly adopt after you have played for some time (see page 93).

With 8 points or more, responder has a chance for game opposite 1NT and therefore must not make a weak suit response at the 2-level. 2NT is used as a response with exactly 8-9 points (see Chapter 3) and the Stayman Convention (see page 93) can also be used when exploring for game in a major suit with 8 points or more. Other strong responses to 1NT are covered in Chapter 5.

OPENER'S REBIDS AFTER A WEAK RESPONSE

Opener's hand is generally divided into three ranges :

13-15 points : **Minimum opening**
16-18 points : **Strong opening**
19 points up : **Maximum opening**

Strategy : If the partnership may hold 26 points, keep on bidding since game is feasible. If the combined total is 25 points at least and there might be more, bid for a game. If the combined total is 25 points at most and there might be less, do not bid for a game. With 26 points together, game is a good bet; with 25 points together, game is a fair bet and with 24 points or less together, game is a poor bet. This bidding strategy is revealed in the approach taken by opener after a weak response from partner.

Opener's action after a raise to the 2-level (e.g. 1♡ : 2♡, . . . ?)

Count HCP plus 5-3-1 shortages (void 5, singleton 3, doubleton 1).

13-15 points **Pass** (responder has 6-9 = no 26 points.)

16-18 points **Bid again** (raise a major to the 3-level; if your suit is a minor, raise to the 3-level or try 2NT.)

19 points up **Bid game** (if your suit is a major, raise it to the 4-level; if it is a minor, consider 3NT if your hand is balanced or semi-balanced.)

After a 1NT response (e.g. 1◊ : 1NT, . . . ?)

(a) If satisfied with no-trumps :

13-15 points **Pass** (responder has 6-9 = no 26 points)

16-18 points **2NT** (opener figures to be semi-balanced)

19 points up **3NT** (the partnership has 25 points at worst)

(b) If not happy with no-trumps :

13-15 points Bid a new suit lower than your first bid suit *or* repeat your first suit with extra length in the suit.

16-18 points Bid any new suit *or* with no second suit, jump to three in the first suit with 6 cards in it.

19 points up Jump to the 3-level in a new suit (jump-shift) *or* jump to game in your suit.

♠ A 9 8 4 3   You opened 1♠. Your rebid after 2♠ or 1NT?
♡ A 9 7   Over 2♠ you should pass — the partnership does not have
◊ K Q   26 points. Pass also over 1NT — with a 5-3-3-2 pattern,
♣ J 3 2   the shape is balanced, so no-trumps is attractive.

♠ 7   You opened 1♡. Your rebid after 2♡ or 1NT?
♡ A 9 7 3 2   Over 2♡, you should pass — no 26 points, but over
◊ K Q 8 6   1NT, prefer to rebid 2◊ — your hand is unbalanced and
♣ Q J 4   so a trump contract figures to be a better chance.

♠ A Q 8 6 4   You opened 1♠. Your rebid after 2♠ or 1NT?
♡ A K 9 3   You have more than 20 points and therefore enough for
◊ A Q   game opposite partner's 6-9 points. Over 2♠, bid 4♠.
♣ J 7   Over 1NT, force to game with a jump-shift to 3♡.

♠ 9   You opened 1◊. Your rebid after 2◊ or 1NT?
♡ K Q 8   Game is possible but not certain. In both cases,
◊ A K 8 7 4 3   rebid 3◊ to invite game. Responder will pass if minimum,
♣ A 9 3   but will bid again with a maximum (8-9 points).

After a suit response at the 1-level (e.g. 1♣ : 1♡, . . . ?)

(a) Opener has 13-15 points

With a minimum opening, opener makes a minimum rebid. You must not make a jump rebid as opener unless you have a strong hand. In order of preference, opener's possible rebids are :

●   **Raise responder's suit.** This requires 4-card support since the suit bid by responder need not have more than four cards in it. The only time opener would not raise responder's suit at once is if the bidding has begun 1♣ : 1◊ and opener has a 4-card major as well as support for diamonds. Show your major first rather than support partner's minor.

●   **Bid a new suit at the 1-level.** The new suit must have four cards in it, but any suit quality will do for a rebid. Prefer to bid a new suit at the 1-level to rebidding with 1NT or repeating your first suit.

●   **Rebid 1NT if your hand is balanced.**

●   **Bid a new suit at the 2-level lower than your first suit.** With a minimum opening, you should not rebid higher than two of your first suit unless you are supporting responder's suit.

●   **Rebid your first suit as a last resort.** To rebid your suit after a 1-level response, the suit must have extra length (more than the opening promised).

(b) Opener has 16-18 points

In order of preference, opener should : ₍

Jump-raise responder's suit to the 3-level. Opener must have 4-card support for this. The only time opener would not raise responder at once is if the bidding has begun 1♣ : 1◇, and opener has a 4-card major as well as support for diamonds. In that case, show the major first.

Bid a new suit at the 1-level or 2-level.

As a last resort, jump to the 3-level in the suit opened, provided that you have at least six cards in that suit.

(c) Opener has 19 points or more

In order of preference, opener should :

Jump to game in responder's suit. This requires 4-card support. The only time opener would not support responder at once is if the bidding has begun 1♣ : 1◇, and opener has a 4-card major as well as support for diamonds. In that case, opener would jump-shift to two of the major rather than support the diamonds yet. Majors come first.

Jump to 2NT, provided that your hand is balanced. After a minor suit opening, the jump to 2NT (e.g. 1♣ : 1♡, 2NT) is forcing to game.

Jump-shift (i.e. make a jump bid in a new suit). The jump-shift denies a balanced hand but is forcing to game as it promises 19 points up.

As a last resort, if none of the above is available, jump to game in your first suit, provided you have a very powerful 6-card suit (it should contain at least four honors) or a strong 7-card suit.

♠ Q 8	You opened 1◇. Your rebid over 1♡ or 1♠?
♡ 4	In either case you should rebid 2♣, showing your
◇ A J 8 7 3	second suit and denying a balanced hand (no NT rebid).
♣ A Q J 6 2	Further action will depend on responder's rebid.

♠ A K 3	You opened 1♣. Your rebid after 1◇, 1♡ or 1♠?
♡ A Q 4	In each case you should rebid with a jump to 2NT, showing
◇ A 9 8	a balanced 19-21 points and forcing to game. Responder
♣ Q 10 3 2	may raise to 3NT, suggest a suit contract or aim for slam.

♠ A 7 3 2	You opened 1◇. Your rebid after 1♡ or 1♠?
♡ 6	Over 1♡, rebid 1♠ and not 2◇ − show a major rather
◇ A Q J 9 5	than rebid a longer minor. Over 1♠, you are worth 17 points
♣ K 8 3	(via the singleton) so that you should jump-raise to 3♠.

RESPONDER'S REBID WITH A WEAK RESPONDING HAND

If the opener has made a minimum rebid, confirming a hand in the 13-15 point range, responder is allowed to pass. However, responder is not obliged to pass if opener's rebid is unsuitable, but responder with a weak hand must not make a strong rebid. Responder is entitled to bid again with a weak hand, provided that responder's rebid is :

● **A raise of opener's second suit** (e.g. 1♣ : 1♡, 1♠ : 2♠). This still shows just 6-9 points in the same way that an immediate raise (1♠ : 2♠) shows 6-9 points. Four trumps are needed to raise opener's second suit.

● **A preference to opener's first suit** (e.g. 1◇ : 1♡, 1♠ : 2◇). This also shows just 6-9 points in the same way that an immediate raise of opener's first suit (1◇ : 2◇) shows 6-9 points.

● **A rebid of 1NT shows 6-9 points in the same way that an initial response of 1NT shows 6-9 points.**

● **As a last resort, responder may rebid his own suit, provided that it contains at least six cards or is a strong 5-card suit.**

If the opener's rebid is a jump showing 16-18 points, the responder is permitted to pass with just 6-7 points but is expected to bid on with 8 points or more since the partnership could then have 26 points or better.

If opener's rebid is a change of suit, opener may have up to 18 points (opener's range for a change of suit is 13-18 since 19 points or more are needed for a jump-shift rebid). Accordingly, responder strives to find a rebid with 8 points or better, since the partnership could have 26 points.

If opener's rebid is a jump showing 19 points or more (a jump-shift or a jump to 2NT or a jump to game), responder is forced to bid again if game has not yet been reached, but is permitted to pass, of course, if opener's rebid is already a game (e.g. 1♡ : 1♠, 4♡).

♠ A J 8 7 6	If partner opened 1◇ and you responded 1♠, then if
♡ 7 3 2	partner rebids 1NT, 2◇ or 2♠, you should pass, but if partner
◇ K 5 4	rebids 2♣, you should rebid 2◇ — show a preference for one
♣ 8 6	of partner's suits rather than rebid an ordinary 5-card suit.

♠ A 10 9 7 3 2	If partner opened 1◇ and you responded 1♠, then if
♡ Q 4	partner rebids 1NT, 2◇ or 2♡, you should rebid 2♠,
◇ 2	showing long spades but a minimum response (6-9 points)
♣ 8 7 5 3	but if partner rebids 2NT or 3♠, you should rebid 4♠.

PARTNERSHIP BIDDING PRACTICE
FEATURING RESPONDING WITH WEAK HANDS

West is the dealer on each hand. How should the bidding go?

WEST	EAST	WEST	EAST
9.	**9.**	**15.**	**15.**
♠ K Q 7 4	♠ 6 5	♠ K 7 2	♠ A J
♡ A 8	♡ K J 5 2	♡ A 8 3	♡ K Q 9 7 2
◊ 9 7 3	◊ A 8 6 4	◊ Q 9 5	◊ A J 6 2
♣ A 7 6 2	♣ 8 4 3	♣ 9 6 5 3	♣ 8 7
10.	**10.**	**16.**	**16.**
♠ A J 8	♠ 4	♠ A K 8 7 2	♠ 4 3
♡ K Q 3	♡ J 10 8 6 5	♡ K Q J	♡ 9 6 5
◊ A J 4	◊ K Q 5	◊ A 9	◊ K Q 7 4
♣ K Q 7 2	♣ 8 6 4 3	♣ 8 6 4	♣ K J 10 5
11.	**11.**	**17.**	**17.**
♠ 8 4 3	♠ A 9 7 2	♠ Q 10 5	♠ A 8 4
♡ A 6 2	♡ K Q 4	♡ Q J 6	♡ K 9 2
◊ K 5	◊ A 8	◊ 8 2	◊ K Q 7 6 5
♣ 10 9 7 6 2	♣ K Q J 3	♣ K 9 5 4 3	♣ 8 2
12.	**12.**	**18.**	**18.**
♠ A Q 9 5	♠ 6 3	♠ A 8 6 3	♠ 5 4
♡ K Q 7 3	♡ J 6 5 2	♡ 8 4	♡ K Q 9 7
◊ 8 6	◊ A K 4 3	◊ A 10 6 5	◊ K 7 4 2
♣ K 7 2	♣ 9 8 5	♣ K 3 2	♣ 7 6 5
13.	**13.**	**19.**	**19.**
♠ 9 7 6 4 2	♠ A K 5 3	♠ Q 8 3 2	♠ J 9 7 4
♡ 7 5	♡ A 9 3	♡ K Q 9 5	♡ 7 4 3
◊ A 8 5 4	◊ 6	◊ 9 4	◊ A Q
♣ J 9	♣ A K 8 4 3	♣ 8 4 3	♣ K Q J 6
14.	**14.**	**20.**	**20.**
♠ A J 8 7 6	♠ 5 2	♠ A J 7 5	♠ K 9 8 3
♡ A K Q 3	♡ J 9 7 6	♡ 4	♡ 8 7 6 5 2
◊ A J	◊ K 6 4 3	◊ K 4 3	◊ Q J 5
♣ 7 6	♣ K 8 4	♣ A K Q 6 2	♣ 4

PLAY HANDS ON WEAK RESPONDING HANDS

Hand 9 : Drawing trumps — Discarding a loser on dummy's winner

Dealer North : Nil vulnerable

NORTH
♠ A K Q 9 8 3
♡ A 8 6
◇ Q 3
♣ J 10

WEST
♠ 10 2
♡ 4
◇ K 10 7 6
♣ 8 7 6 5 4 2

EAST
♠ J
♡ K Q J 10 5 3
◇ A 9 8 2
♣ 9 3

SOUTH
♠ 7 6 5 4
♡ 9 7 2
◇ J 5 4
♣ A K Q

WEST	NORTH	EAST	SOUTH
	1♠	2♡	2♠
Pass	3♠	Pass	4♠
Pass	Pass	Pass	

Bidding: North's 3♠ invites South to bid game with 8+ points.

Lead : ♡ K, top of sequence.

Play: South wins ♡ A, draws trumps in two rounds and plays A-K-Q of clubs to discard a red suit loser. It is normal to draw trumps first.

Wrong play: (1) Failing to win the ♡ A at trick one. West would ruff the next heart and could defeat 4♠. (2) Playing clubs before drawing trumps. East ruffs the third round of clubs and 4♠ would be beaten.

Hand 10 : Drawing trumps — Setting up winners to discard a loser

Dealer East : N-S vulnerable

NORTH
♠ 10 6
♡ 8 2
◇ 9 8 4 3
♣ K 10 6 4 2

WEST
♠ K J 9 8
♡ 6 5 4
◇ J 5
♣ J 8 7 3

EAST
♠ A Q 4 3
♡ A K 7
◇ K Q 10 7 2
♣ 9

SOUTH
♠ 7 5 2
♡ Q J 10 9 3
◇ A 6
♣ A Q 5

WEST	NORTH	EAST	SOUTH
		1◇	1♡
1♠	Pass	4♠	All pass

Bidding : West is worth the 1♠ response and East revalues to 21 points, counting 3 for the singleton since support is held for West's suit.

Lead : ♡ 8. Lead partner's suit. From a doubleton, lead the top card.

Play: Win the ♡ A. Draw trumps in three rounds. Then play the jack of diamonds to knock out the ace and thereby setting up the other diamonds as winners. When the lead is regained, play the diamonds and discard a heart loser and two clubs. Losing just one diamond and one club, 11 tricks.

Hand 11 : Ruffing a loser in dummy — Delaying drawing trumps

Dealer South : Both vulnerable

NORTH
♠ 5 3
♡ 9 2
◇ K Q 9 3
♣ J 8 7 4 2

WEST
♠ Q J 10 8
♡ Q J 5
◇ 5 4 2
♣ K 6 3

EAST
♠ 7 6 4 2
♡ 10 7
◇ A J 10 8
♣ A 10 9

SOUTH
♠ A K 9
♡ A K 8 6 4 3
◇ 7 6
♣ Q 5

WEST	NORTH	EAST	SOUTH
			1♡
Pass	1NT	Pass	3♡
Pass	Pass	Pass	

Bidding : South's 3♡ shows six hearts and 16-18 points, inviting North to bid game with more than just 6-7 points.

Lead : ♠Q. Top of sequence.

Play: South should win and play the other spade winner, followed by the third spade, ruffed in dummy. Then, the A-K of hearts should be followed by a diamond to the king.

Wrong play : Failing to ruff the spade loser in dummy. If South plays A-K of hearts at once, dummy is unable to ruff a spade and there are 5 losers.

Hand 12 : Urgent discard of a loser — Delaying drawing trumps

Dealer West : Nil vulnerable

NORTH
♠ 5 4
♡ 8 6
◇ A 10 9 3 2
♣ 10 7 5 4

WEST
♠ A 9 8
♡ K 4 2
◇ Q J 8
♣ A K Q 3

EAST
♠ 7 3 2
♡ Q J 10 9 5
◇ K 7 6
♣ 6 2

SOUTH
♠ K Q J 10 6
♡ A 7 3
◇ 5 4
♣ J 9 8

WEST	NORTH	EAST	SOUTH
1♣	Pass	1♡	1♠
2NT	Pass	3♡	Pass
4♡	Pass	Pass	Pass

Bidding : West, too strong to open 1NT, makes a jump-rebid in NT. East repeats the hearts to show five, asking West to choose 4♡ or 3NT.

Lead : ♠K. Top of sequence.

Play : Win ♠A. Play ♣A-K-Q to discard one spade loser. Then lead trumps. When the lead is regained, draw the missing trumps, followed by diamonds to knock out the ◇ A. Lose 1 spade, 1 heart and 1 diamond. Do not lead trumps before taking a discard on dummy's clubs. Do not lead the fourth round of clubs.

CHAPTER 5
RESPONDING WITH STRONG HANDS

RESPONDING TO AN OPENING OF 1♣, 1◇, 1♡ OR 1♠

Hands with 10 or more high card points are considered strong hands for responder. Hands with exactly 10 hcp are borderline. With 10 hcp and a 4-3-3-3 pattern, the 1NT response would be acceptable. Other patterns with exactly 10 hcp would be too strong for 1NT. Hands with 10 hcp and 4-3-3-3 pattern would be acceptable for the weak raise of opener's suit to the 2-level, provided that trump support is present. Other patterns with 10 hcp would be too strong.

Responder's most common action with a strong hand is to change suit, await further information from opener and then either make a decision as to the best contract or make another descriptive bid to help partner. When responder is changing suit, the normal order of priorities applies:

Bid your longest suit first.

With 5-5 or 6-6 patterns, bid the higher ranking suit first.

4-card suits are bid up-the-line.

Since responder has a strong hand, there will not be any need to bid the suits out of natural order (in the way that responder might have to bid suits in a different order with a weak hand — see page 28). When bidding a new suit, responder may bid at the 1-level or the 2-level. A new suit at the 1-level shows 6 points or more, while a new suit at the 2-level shows 10 points or more, provided that it is not a jump-shift. When bidding a new suit, responder will bid it at the cheapest possible level and a suit response at the 1-level does not deny a strong hand. If responder does jump-shift (e.g. 1♣ : 2♡ *or* 1♠ : 3♣), responder shows 19 points or more and usually a powerful 5-card or longer suit. The jump-shift is a very rare response but when it occurs, it is forcing to game and strongly suggests slam possibilities.

Aside from changing suit, responder has three specific strong responses, but the hand must fit the requirements before these bids are chosen :

2NT response — 13-15 points, balanced shape, stoppers in unbid suits.

3NT response — 16-18 points, balanced shape, stoppers in unbid suits.

Jump-raise, e.g. 1♠ : 3♠ — 13 points or more and strong support.

The 2NT and 3NT responses are not all that common but if the hand fits, prefer that response to a change of suit. The minimum holdings which qualify as stoppers are A-x, K-x, Q-x-x or J-x-x-x.

Responder's general strategy of developing a strong hand :

10-12 points: Respond with a change of suit and then bid again, inviting game. For example, 1♠ : 2♣, 2◊ : 3◊ ... *or* 1♠ : 2♣, 2◊ : 3♣ ... *or* 1♡ : 2♣ : 2◊ : 2♡ ...

13-15 points: These hands are strong enough to bid for a game. If the hand fits 2NT or a jump-raise, choose that response. If not, change suit and bid game on the next round if you know the best spot *or* change suit again which will require the opener to bid once more *or* jump on the next round. For example, 1◊ : 1♠, 1NT : 4♠ ... *or* 1♡ : 2♣, 2♡ : 4♡ ...

16-18 points: Choose the 3NT response or a jump-raise if the hand fits. If not, change suit initially and jump-rebid to insist on game. If opener has confirmed a minimum opening, be content with game but if opener has promised better than minimum, you should plan to look for a slam.

19 points or more : Jump-shift if possible. If not, change suit and judge which slam to try for after opener has described his hand with the rebid.

An opening hand facing an opening hand should produce a game.

An opening hand facing an opener who jumps can produce a slam if a good trump fit is located. A 19-up hand opposite an opening will usually produce a slam if a good trump fit is located.

RESPONDING TO A 1NT OPENING

With 10 points or more opposite a 1NT opening, game is a good bet. You may jump directly to game if you know the best spot (e.g. 1NT : 3NT *or* 1NT : 4♠) or you may jump to 3-in-a-suit (e.g. 1NT : 3♡) which is forcing to game and shows a 5-card suit. Opener will support your suit if possible, but if opener holds only a doubleton, opener will rebid 3NT. You may also use the Stayman Convention (see page 93) with 8 points or more and a 4-card major. With 8 points or more, game is possible — make sure you do not respond to 1NT with a weak response of 2-in-a-suit which shows only 0-7 points and asks opener to pass. When you have 8 or 9 points only and your long suit is a minor or you have both minor suits, the best bet is stick with no-trumps.

If you have 15 points or more opposite a 1NT opening, you have slam prospects and this is covered in more detail in Chapter 8.

EXAMPLES OF STRONG RESPONDING HANDS

♠ A Q 8 6 4
♡ A K 9 5
◇ 7 3 2
♣ 5

Suppose partner opened 1♣. You know you have enough for game, but which game? As you cannot tell, respond 1♠ and await opener's rebid. If opener rebids 2♠, bid 4♠, but over 2♣, bid 2♡, a new suit, forcing.

♠ A Q 8 6 4 2
♡ A K J
◇ 7 3 2
♣ 5

If partner opened 1♣, respond 1♠. Then, over 2♠, rebid 4♠; over 1NT, rebid 4♠ (opener figures to have two or three spades, since the 1NT rebid should be balanced); over 2♣, rebid 3♠ (a jump rebid is forcing).

♠ A J 5
♡ Q 9 6
◇ K J 8
♣ Q J 9 4

If partner opens the bidding, you have enough for a game, no matter which opening bid was chosen. Over any suit opening, you should respond 2NT, showing 13-15 balanced. This forces to game and suggests 3NT.

♠ 8
♡ A 9 8 5 4
◇ A Q 7 4 3
♣ J 2

If partner opened 1♠, respond 2♡, the higher suit with a 5-5 pattern. Responder's change of suit normally promises no more than a 4-card suit. However, 1♠ : 2♡ is an exception and *promises five hearts*.

♠ A 7 5 2
♡ 5
◇ A J 6 3
♣ A Q 9 4

If partner opened 1♡, respond 1♠. 4-card suits are bid up-the-line. 'Cheapest' does not mean 'lowest' : 1♠ is cheaper than 2♣. It would be an error to respond 2NT, since that would guarantee a balanced hand.

♠ A J 8
♡ 8 7
◇ Q J 6 4
♣ K 9 8 3

Hands of 11-12 points can be awkward to bid. Over a 1♣ opening, respond 1◇ and over a 1◇ opening, bid 2♣. You are too strong to raise to the 2-level. Over 1♡ or 1♠, respond 2♣, up-the-line.

♠ A K Q J 7 4
♡ A K 8
◇ 8 7
♣ Q 2

If partner opened 1♣, 1◇ or 1♡, you should respond 2♠, a jump-shift showing 19 or more points and forcing to game, as well as a strong suggestion of slam values. The jump-shift is usually a strong 5-card or longer suit.

♠ 8 5
♡ A Q 4 2
◇ A 8 7
♣ K J 5 4

If partner opened 1♠, your hand is ideal for a 2NT response, while over 1♡, you would jump-raise to 3♡. Over 1♣ or 1◇, the spades are too weak for a response of 2NT. In either case, it is best to bid just 1♡ initially.

EXERCISES ON RESPONDING WITH A STRONG HAND

A. Partner opens 1♣, next player passes. What is your response?

	1.	2.	3.	4.
♠	K Q 8	K Q 8	8 7 4	K Q 8
♡	A J 7	A J 7	A J 7	A J 7 4 2
◇	K 9 7 2	K 9 7 2	K 9 7 2	K 9
♣	8 4 3	A 8 4	A Q 3	J 8 3

	5.	6.	7.	8.
♠	A J 8 2	A J 8 2	A J 8 2	7 6
♡	A J 7 6	A J 7 6	7	A Q J 4
◇	A Q 7 4	7	A Q 7 4	A K 9
♣	7	A Q 7 4	A J 7 6	A Q 3 2

B. Partner opens 1◇, next player passes. What is your response?

	1.	2.	3.	4.
♠	A 7	A 7	A Q 8 4	A Q 8 4 3
♡	A 9 7	A 9 7 2	K Q 7 2	K Q 7 3 2
◇	Q J 8 4 3	Q J 8 4 3	K 3	K 3
♣	Q 9 4	K 6	7 6 5	5

C. Partner opens 1♡, next player passes. What is your response?

	1.	2.	3.	4.
♠	A Q 9 8	A Q 9 8	8 4 3	8 4
♡	K Q 7 2	K 7 2	K 3	3
◇	K 3	K Q 3 2	Q J 7 6	A Q 9 7 6
♣	7 6 3	7 6	A J 9 8	A K 8 4 3

D. Partner opens 1♠, next player passes. What is your response?

	1.	2.	3.	4.
♠	A J 7	A J 7	7 4	Q 8 4 3
♡	6 4 2	K Q 9 3 2	A Q 8 6	K 8
◇	K Q 9 3	K 7	A K 9 3	A J 6 3
♣	J 8 7	8 4 2	8 4 2	J 6 2

E. Partner opens 1NT, next player passes. What is your response?

	1.	2.	3.	4.
♠	K Q 8 7 6	A 7	4	4
♡	A 8	K J 8	K J 8 7 3 2	K Q 9 5 3
◇	J 6 3 2	Q 9 8 7 3 2	A 9 8	A Q 7 6 4
♣	J 8	8 6	Q 6 2	A 3

OPENER'S REBIDS AFTER A STRONG RESPONSE

After a suit response at the 1-level

A suit response at the 1-level can be a weak responding hand or a strong responding hand. Opener's rebids have been discussed on pages 31-33.

After a response of 2NT or 3NT or a jump-raise

Opener should bid no higher than game with a minimum opening and explore slam possibilities with a powerful opening. Slam bidding is covered in Chapter 8. Where the response was 2NT or 3NT, opener will stay with no-trumps with a balanced hand, but will try to play in a trump contract if the hand is unbalanced. For example, after 1♠ : 2NT, opener could rebid 3♡ to show five spades and four hearts and a desire to play in one of the majors rather than no-trumps.

After a jump-shift response

Opener should support responder's suit with three or more trumps. Without support, make a natural rebid, bidding a second suit if possible.

After a suit response at the 2-level (e.g. 1♡ : 2♣)

With a minimum opening, your order of priorities are :

● Support responder to the 3-level (e.g. 1♡ : 2♣, 3♣). Opener would choose not to support responder at once only after 1♠ : 2♣ or 1♠ : 2◇, when opener with four hearts would rather bid 2♡ to show the other major.

● Bid a new suit, lower-ranking than the first suit (e.g. 1♡ : 2♣, 2◇).

● Repeat the first suit with at least 5 cards in the suit (e.g. 1♡ : 2♣, 2♡). The suit need not be more than five cards long — the rebid of opener's first suit is used to confirm a minimum opening with no cheaper suit to bid.

● Rebid 2NT with a balanced hand. 1◇ : 2♣, 2NT is used to show a minimum opening hand (weaker than a 1NT opening), but a 2NT rebid after opening 1♡ or 1♠ is strong, 15-18 HCP. It aims to show the 1NT opening with a 5-card major in a 5-3-3-2 pattern.

Opener's change of suit to a lower suit (e.g. 1♠ : 2◇, 2♡) has a range of 13-18 points, since a jump-shift needs 19 points or more. It may thus be a minimum opening or a strong opening and so change-of-suit after a 2-level response is forcing. A new suit by opener beyond 2-in-the-suit-opened (e.g. 1◇ : 2♣, 2♡) shows better than a minimum opening. It is therefore forcing to game since responder has 10 points or more for the 2-level response and opener has 16 points or more for a strong rebid.

EXERCISES ON REBIDS AFTER A STRONG RESPONSE

A. West 1♢ : East 2NT. West's rebid?

1.	♠ K 7	2.	♠ 7	3.	♠ 6	4.	♠ A 7 2
	♡ 8 4 3		♡ K Q 4 3		♡ 5 4		♡ 6 5 3
	♢ A Q 6 5 4		♢ A K J 6 2		♢ A K J 8 6		♢ K Q 9 8
	♣ K J 4		♣ 9 4 2		♣ A Q J 6 3		♣ A 4 3

B. West 1♢ : East 2♣. West's rebid?

1.	♠ K Q 3	2.	♠ K Q 3	3.	♠ K 3 2	4.	♠ 7 2
	♡ A 8 7		♡ A 8 7		♡ A J 8 6		♡ A 2
	♢ K J 7 4		♢ K Q J 4		♢ K Q 9 8 7		♢ A Q 8 7 4
	♣ 8 6 2		♣ A 10 7		♣ 4		♣ K 4 3 2

C. West 1♡ : East 2♣. West's rebid?

1.	♠ A 4	2.	♠ A 9 8 3	3.	♠ 9 7 4	4.	♠ Q 8
	♡ K Q 7 6 2		♡ K Q 7 6 2		♡ A K J 7 2		♡ A J 9 7 4 2
	♢ A 9 8 3		♢ 7 6		♢ 9 7 2		♢ K Q 5
	♣ 7 6		♣ A 4		♣ A 3		♣ J 8

5.	♠ A J 8	6.	♠ A J 8	7.	♠ A J 8 2	8.	♠ 7 2
	♡ A Q 7 6 4		♡ A Q 7 6 4		♡ A Q J 9 5 2		♡ A 9 7 3 2
	♢ K 7 4		♢ K Q 4		♢ A 4		♢ A K Q 5
	♣ K 2		♣ K 7 4		♣ 3		♣ A 8

D. West 1♡ : East 2NT. West's rebid?

1.	♠ A J 7 4	2.	♠ A J 7	3.	♠ A 6	4.	♠ - - -
	♡ K J 9 5 4		♡ K J 9 8 4 3		♡ A 9 7 5 3		♡ A Q 8 6 4
	♢ 7		♢ 7		♢ K Q 3		♢ K Q 7 6 3
	♣ A 4 3		♣ K J 2		♣ 7 6 2		♣ Q J 8

E. West 1♠ : East 2♢. West's rebid?

1.	♠ A K 9 8 3	2.	♠ A K 9 8 3	3.	♠ A K J 7 3 2	4.	♠ A Q J 9 8 6 2
	♡ K Q 7 6		♡ 8 4 3		♡ A 4 3		♡ 7 2
	♢ 4		♢ 4		♢ 9 2		♢ K Q J
	♣ 8 4 3		♣ K Q 7 6		♣ K Q		♣ J

PARTNERSHIP BIDDING PRACTICE
FEATURING RESPONDING WITH STRONG HANDS

West is the dealer on each hand. How should the bidding go?

WEST	EAST	WEST	EAST
21.	**21.**	**27.**	**27.**
♠ A J 9 7	♠ 8 2	♠ A J 8	♠ K 7 2
♡ K 9 4	♡ A Q 7 2	♡ K Q 7	♡ 9 5
◇ 7 6	◇ K 9 4 3	◇ K 9 4 2	◇ 8 5 3
♣ A J 3 2	♣ K Q 6	♣ 7 6 2	♣ A K 8 4 3
22.	**22.**	**28.**	**28.**
♠ A Q J 7 3	♠ 8 2	♠ A 7	♠ 9 4 3
♡ 4	♡ A Q 7 2	♡ 7 2	♡ K J 8 4
◇ 7	◇ K 9 4 3	◇ K Q J 5 3	◇ A 7
♣ A J 9 5 4 3	♣ K Q 6	♣ A Q 10 6	♣ K 5 3 2
23.	**23.**	**29.**	**29.**
♠ A K J	♠ 9 5	♠ A 7 6	♠ K 5
♡ K 7	♡ Q 10 6 5 2	♡ K 8 4 3	♡ Q J 6 5
◇ 7 2	◇ A K J 9	◇ K Q 9 6 2	◇ 8 7
♣ A J 9 8 4 3	♣ 6 2	♣ 8	♣ A K 9 4 3
24.	**24.**	**30.**	**30.**
♠ J 6	♠ 9 5	♠ A 6	♠ 7 2
♡ K J 3	♡ Q 10 6 5 2	♡ 4 3	♡ K Q J 8 5 2
◇ Q 7	◇ A K J 9	◇ A Q 8 7 4	◇ J 6
♣ A J 9 8 4 3	♣ K 2	♣ K Q J 3	♣ A 5 2
25.	**25.**	**31.**	**31.**
♠ 7 6 4 3	♠ A J 9 2	♠ K Q 6	♠ A 8 4 3
♡ A Q 8 7	♡ 4 2	♡ 7 2	♡ A 10 5 3
◇ 6	◇ A K 9 7 5	◇ A Q 9 7 5 3	◇ K 4
♣ A K 4 3	♣ 8 6	♣ J 8	♣ K 9 2
26.	**26.**	**32.**	**32.**
♠ Q J 3	♠ K 4	♠ 7	♠ A K 8 4 3
♡ A Q 8 7	♡ 6 2	♡ J 2	♡ K Q 9 4
◇ 6	◇ A K J 8 7 5	◇ A J 7 6 2	◇ 5 3
♣ A K 5 4 3	♣ 9 7	♣ A Q 9 7 5	♣ J 6

PARTNERSHIP BIDDING PRACTICE
FEATURING RESPONDING WITH STRONG HANDS

West is the dealer on each hand. How should the bidding go?

WEST	EAST	WEST	EAST
33.	**33.**	**39.**	**39.**
♠ 8 6 5	♠ A K 9 4 2	♠ A K J 8 7	♠ 6 5 4
♡ A Q 7 4 3 2	♡ 6	♡ A Q J 6 3	♡ 8 5
◇ A K 9	◇ Q 8 3	◇ 7 3	◇ A K 8 6 2
♣ 2	♣ Q J 10 5	♣ 8	♣ K 7 2
34.	**34.**	**40.**	**40.**
♠ 8	♠ A K 9 4 2	♠ A K J 8 7	♠ 6
♡ A Q 7 4 3 2	♡ 6	♡ A Q J 6 5	♡ K 8 4
◇ A K 9	◇ Q 8 3	◇ 7 3	◇ A Q 8 6 4
♣ 8 6 2	♣ Q J 10 5	♣ 8	♣ Q 9 7 2
35.	**35.**	**41.**	**41.**
♠ A J 9	♠ Q 8 2	♠ A K J 8 7	♠ 9 6
♡ K Q 8 4 3	♡ J 5	♡ A Q J 6	♡ K 8
◇ A Q 4 2	◇ J 8 7	◇ 7 3	◇ A Q 8 6 4
♣ 6	♣ A K 8 7 3	♣ 8 5	♣ Q 9 7 2
36.	**36.**	**42.**	**42.**
♠ K 9 5 2	♠ 8 6 3	♠ K Q 6 5 4	♠ 8
♡ A K J 8 7	♡ Q	♡ A 2	♡ K Q 8 7 6 3
◇ Q 3 2	◇ A 6 5	◇ A Q 9 8 3	◇ K J 6
♣ K	♣ A Q 8 6 5 2	♣ Q	♣ J 7 2
37.	**37.**	**43.**	**43.**
♠ A K J 2	♠ Q 7 6 5 4	♠ A Q 8 7 4	♠ J 6
♡ K 9 7 6 4	♡ 5 3	♡ J 6	♡ A 8 7 4 3
◇ J 2	◇ A K 9 4 3	◇ K Q J	◇ A 9 5
♣ 6 3	♣ 4	♣ 9 8 3	♣ J 4 2
38.	**38.**	**44.**	**44.**
♠ 6	♠ Q 8 7	♠ A Q 8 7 4	♠ J 6
♡ A Q J 7 6	♡ 8 3 2	♡ J 6 2	♡ A K 8 4 3
◇ K Q J 5	◇ A 9 8 3 2	◇ K Q J	◇ A 9 5
♣ 9 3 2	♣ A J	♣ 9 8	♣ J 6 4

PLAY HANDS ON STRONG RESPONDING HANDS

Hand 13 : Coping with a bad break — The marked finesse

Dealer North : Nil vulnerable

NORTH
- ♠ 10 7 4
- ♡ A K Q 10
- ◇ K
- ♣ J 8 7 6 2

WEST
- ♠ A K 8 6 3
- ♡ J 9 8 2
- ◇ A 9
- ♣ Q 9

EAST
- ♠ 9 5 2
- ♡ - - -
- ◇ 10 8 7 6 5 4
- ♣ 10 5 4 3

SOUTH
- ♠ Q J
- ♡ 7 6 5 4 3
- ◇ Q J 3 2
- ♣ A K

WEST	NORTH	EAST	SOUTH
	1♣	Pass	1♡
1♠	2♡	Pass	4♡
Pass	Pass	Pass	

Bidding : With 13 points opposite an opening, South always intended to reach game. When North raised hearts, that settled the matter.

Lead : ♠K, normal from A-K suits.

Play : After the top spades and the ◇ A, win the next trick and play the ♡A. When East shows out, play a club to hand and lead a heart towards dummy, *finessing* the 10 when West plays low. Draw West's trumps and use the ♠10 or the ♣J to discard a diamond loser.

Hand 14 : Drawing trumps — The marked finesse

Dealer East : N-S vulnerable

NORTH
- ♠ - - -
- ♡ 10 8 5 4
- ◇ A 7 5 3
- ♣ 8 7 4 3 2

WEST
- ♠ A K J 5
- ♡ J 7 3 2
- ◇ K J 4
- ♣ J 6

EAST
- ♠ 9 7 6 4 3 2
- ♡ A K Q
- ◇ Q 9
- ♣ Q 9

SOUTH
- ♠ Q 10 8
- ♡ 9 6
- ◇ 10 8 6 2
- ♣ A K 10 5

WEST	NORTH	EAST	SOUTH
		1♠	Pass
3♠	Pass	4♠	All pass

Bidding : West's jump raise shows 13 points or more plus trump support.

Lead : ♣K, normal from A-K suits.

Play : South switches to a red suit after cashing the top clubs. When East gets in, East leads a spade to the ace and, on North's showing out, calculates that South started with Q-10-8 in trumps and still has Q-x. To capture the queen, East returns to hand with a heart and leads a spade, finessing dummy's jack. The last trump is drawn and East loses at most one diamond and two clubs.

Hand 15 : Drawing trumps in the correct order — The marked finesse

Dealer South: Both vulnerable

	WEST	NORTH	EAST	SOUTH
				1♣
	1◇	1♡	Pass	2♡
	Pass	4♡	All pass	

NORTH
♠ A 9 7 5
♡ K Q 4 2
◇ 8 5 2
♣ K Q

WEST
♠ Q J 4
♡ 9
◇ A K Q 10 7
♣ 8 6 4 2

EAST
♠ 10 8 6 3 2
♡ J 8 6 5
◇ 9 4
♣ 7 5

SOUTH
♠ K
♡ A 10 7 3
◇ J 6 3
♣ A J 10 9 3

Bidding : 1♡ was up-the-line.

Lead : ◇ 9. Partner's suit is first choice. High-low with a doubleton.

Play: After 3 diamond tricks and a black suit exit, play off K-Q of hearts first (keep the A-10 tenace intact) and when West discards, finesse against East's jack, thus not losing a heart trick. If trumps were 3-2, the order of playing the top trumps would not matter. K-Q first caters for East's holding J-x-x-x. Had West continued with a fourth diamond, a careful North would ruff this in hand.

Hand 16 : Drawing trumps — Marked finesse — Repeating the finesse

Dealer West : Nil vulnerable

WEST	NORTH	EAST	SOUTH
Pass	Pass	1NT	Pass
4♠	Pass	Pass	Pass

NORTH
♠ - - -
♡ 10 9 6 3 2
◇ 9 7 5 4 2
♣ A K 8

WEST
♠ A J 10 7 4 3
♡ K 8 4
◇ J 10
♣ 6 3

EAST
♠ K 5 2
♡ Q J 7
◇ A K Q
♣ J 9 4 2

SOUTH
♠ Q 9 8 6
♡ A 5
◇ 8 6 3
♣ Q 10 7 5

Bidding: After 1NT, West revalues to 11 points for a spade contract, enough for game opposite 16-18.

Lead : ♣K, normal from A-K suits.

Play: South plays the ♣7 on the king and ♣5 on the ace. High-low on partner's lead is a signal for partner to continue that suit. West ruffs the next club and leads a spade to the king (high-from-shortage). When North shows out, West continues by finessing the jack of spades, leading a diamond to dummy and finessing the ♠10. The ♠A draws South's queen and the heart winners are set up.

CHAPTER 6
BIDDING BY A PASSED HAND

Once you have passed initially, the meaning of some of your bids will be affected, since it is no longer possible for you to hold 13 points, else you would have opened. Your weak responses are not affected: a raise of opener's suit to the 2-level is still 6-9 points and the 1NT response is also still 6-9 points. A change of suit at the 1-level has a range of 6-12 points as opposed to the unlimited nature of the 6 or more points attached to the response of a new suit at the 1-level normally.

The responses with changed meanings are the jump responses and the change of suit to the 2-level. Since a passed hand cannot hold 13 points, a jump response now shows exactly 10-12 points. The specific meanings:

● Jump to 2NT by a passed hand (e.g. Pass : 1♡, 2NT) shows 10-12 points, balanced shape and denies support for opener's suit.

● Jump-raise by a passed hand (e.g. Pass : 1♠, 3♠) shows 10-12 points and support for opener's suit. The shape need not be balanced.

● Jump-shift by a passed hand (e.g. Pass: 1◇, 2♠) shows 10-12 points and a strong 5-card suit. If the suit is only four cards long or if the suit is not strong, bid the suit at the cheapest level without a jump.

The most important rule about bidding by a passed hand is this :

A BID BY A PASSED HAND IS NOT FORCING

This applies whether it is a jump bid or a change of suit so that the normal rules about change-of-suit forcing or jump responses forcing to game do not apply when the responder is a passed hand. Because any bid by a passed hand is not forcing, it is vital to make a response which gives partner the most important message in one bid — there might be no second chance. Therefore, raise a major suit as first priority. Do not bid a new suit when you have a major suit raise available.

The change of suit to the 2-level still requires 10 points, but the range is 10-12 points rather than the normal 10 points or more, and a very significant difference is that a 5-card or longer suit is promised (since it may be passed by opener). With only 4-card suits, bid a suit at the 1-level (a new suit at the 1-level does not promise more than four cards) or respond 1NT or 2NT.

EXERCISES ON PASSED HAND BIDDING

A. You passed as dealer and partner opens 1♣. What is your response?

1.	2.	3.	4.
♠ K Q 6	♠ A J	♠ A Q J 4 3	♠ K 8
♡ K J 8	♡ K Q 3 2	♡ K 9	♡ A Q 9
◇ Q 6 5 2	◇ J 7 6	◇ 7 6 5	◇ 6 3
♣ J 9 4	♣ 8 7 4 2	♣ J 9 2	♣ J 8 7 5 3 2

B. You passed as dealer and partner opens 1♡. What is your response?

1.	2.	3.	4.
♠ A J	♠ A J 8 4 2	♠ K Q 6	♠ A Q J 9 8
♡ K 9 7 6	♡ Q 7 6 2	♡ 4 3	♡ J 6
◇ 6 5 4	◇ 4 3	◇ J 10 4 3	◇ K 4 3
♣ Q J 9 4	♣ 6 2	♣ A J 10 2	♣ 7 6 2

5.	6.	7.	8.
♠ A 9 8 6	♠ A 5 2	♠ A 5 2	♠ 5 2
♡ 7	♡ 4 3	♡ 4	♡ 7 6 4 3
◇ Q 9 8 4	◇ K J 9 8 2	◇ K J 8 2	◇ A K J 8
♣ K J 8 2	♣ Q 4 2	♣ 9 7 5 4 3	♣ Q J 2

PARTNERSHIP BIDDING PRACTICE

West is the dealer on each hand. How should the bidding go?

WEST	EAST	WEST	EAST
45.	**45.**	**48.**	**48.**
♠ A J 7	♠ 9 5	♠ A 7 6 4 2	♠ J 9 8
♡ K 9 8 4	♡ A Q 6 3 2	♡ K J	♡ Q 4 3
◇ 7 6 4 3 2	◇ A K 8	◇ Q 9 8	◇ 6 5 2
♣ 6	♣ J 7 4	♣ J 6 2	♣ A K Q 9
46.	**46.**	**49.**	**49.**
♠ A Q 7 2	♠ K 9 4 3	♠ A J 7	♠ Q 3 2
♡ K 9 8 3	♡ 7	♡ 8 7	♡ K Q 6 2
◇ J 8 7	◇ A K 3	◇ K 8 2	◇ A 7 5
♣ 4 2	♣ A J 9 5 3	♣ K 8 6 4 3	♣ A 9 5
47.	**47.**	**50.**	**50.**
♠ Q 7	♠ K 9 8 5 2	♠ 7	♠ Q J 6 4 3
♡ A 8	♡ K 7 6	♡ A 9 8 2	♡ Q 7
◇ Q J 8 6 4 3	◇ 9 5 2	◇ J 9 7 3	◇ A 8 5
♣ 7 6 2	♣ A Q	♣ A Q 7 6	♣ K 5 2

CHAPTER 7
SUPER-STRONG OPENING BIDS

Hands with more than 21 high card points are too strong to open with a one-opening, since partner will pass that with 5 points or less.

♠ **A K J 8 4 3**   If you were to open this hand with 1♠, imagine your
♡ **A K 3**   dismay if the bidding went — Pass, Pass, Pass. If partner
◊ **A K Q**   held just two or three points, or even less, partner would
♣ **5**   be quite right to pass and yet game is a great chance.

To cope with such powerhouses, open with a Two-Bid. The actual bid chosen will depend on the shape of the hand, but if the hand is not balanced, follow the normal rules: longest suit first; with 5-5 or 6-6 patterns, bid the higher suit first; with 4-card suits only, bid them up-the-line. If the hand is balanced, there are two specific openings to cater for these shapes:

2NT = 22-24 points and balanced shape. Partner is permitted to pass this opening with no points or only one point, but with any chance for game, partner will respond. With a balanced hand, responder keeps to no-trumps, while with unbalanced shapes, bid three-in-a-suit (promises a 5-card suit) or bid game in a major suit with six cards or more in the major. The Stayman 3♣ Convention is also commonly used (see page 93).

3NT = 25-27 points and balanced shape. Responder will stay with 3NT unless there are slam prospects or responder's hand is unbalanced.

Where opener's hand is not balanced, opener may start with 2-in-a-suit on any hand with 22 high card points or more. The hand may contain less than 22 high card points if it is worth more than nine playing tricks.

How to count playing tricks: *In your long suits (four or more cards):* Count the ace and king as winners. Count the queen as a winner if the suit contains another honor. Count every card after the third card as a winner. *In your short suits:* Count A = 1, K with another honor = 1, K with one or more cards but no other honor = ½, Q or J with a higher honor = ½ (but A-K-Q is of course three tricks). For example:

♠ **A K Q 8 7 6 3 2**   This hand is worth 10 tricks with spades as
♡ **A K 5**   trumps. It would be a tragedy to open 1♠ and be
◊ **8**   left there. Open 2♠ and insist on game. To open
♣ **6**   4♠ has a different meaning — see Chapter 9.

RESPONDING TO A 2-OPENING

While responder is expected to pass a one-opening with 0-5 points, *responder must reply to a two-opening,* no matter how weak the hand is. **The two-in-a-suit opening is forcing to game.** This means that both partners must keep bidding until at least game is reached.

Responder's weakest reply is 2NT : 0-7 points and any shape. The 2NT reply is used purely as an artificial, weakness reply because the responder has to make some reply. It need not be a balanced hand at all. If there happens to be an intervening bid over partner's 2-opening, responder would pass to show the negative reply. There is no obligation to bid over an intervening bid, since opener has another chance to bid anyway.

Any response other than 2NT shows a stronger hand, about 8 points or more, about 1½ tricks or better. A positive response often leads to a slam and responder shows support for opener's major suit opening as first option. Responder is entitled to expect the first suit bid by a 2-opener to be a 5-card or longer suit and may therefore support it with just three trumps. If opener repeats the first suit, responder may support it with a doubleton. To support a second suit by opener requires four trumps, however, since the second suit need not have more than four cards. Where responder has a positive reply but not support for opener, the normal rules apply for bidding a new suit (longest first; with 5-5 or 6-6 patterns, bid the higher suit first; 4-card suits up-the-line). With a balanced hand without support for opener, responder may also bid 3NT with about 8-10 high card points. Opener will not pass since slam is likely.

REBIDS BY THE OPENER

(a) After a 2NT response

Opener will bid a second suit of four or more cards as first choice. With no second suit to show, opener will rebid the first suit with six or more cards or rebid 3NT with a 5-3-3-2 pattern. Responder will strive to support opener. If that is not possible, responder may introduce a long suit or rebid 3NT. Responder will not pass the bidding out below game.

(b) After a positive response

Opener will support responder's suit if possible. If not, bid a second suit or rebid the first suit with six or more cards in it. Slam is highly likely after a positive response but it is important to reach agreement on a trump suit if possible. Slam bidding is covered in Chapter 8.

EXERCISES ON SUPER-STRONG OPENING BIDS

A. What is your opening bid on these hands?

1.	♠ A 6	2.	♠ A	3.	♠ A K Q 8 4
	♡ A K J 10 6 2		♡ A K Q		♡ A K J 9 8 7
	◇ A Q		◇ A K J 10 6 5 2		◇ A
	♣ K 8 3		♣ 5 3		♣ 4

4.	♠ Q 7 5 4 3	5.	♠ - - -	6.	♠ A K Q J
	♡ A K 6 5		♡ A K Q 8 6 5 4		♡ A Q J 7
	◇ A K		◇ A Q J 8 7 3		◇ 4
	♣ A 2		♣ - - -		♣ A K Q 8

B. Partner opens 2♡, next player passes. What is your response?

1.	♠ 7 5 4	2.	♠ K 8 7	3.	♠ A 8 7	4.	♠ A 8 7
	♡ 6 4 2		♡ 6 4		♡ 6 4		♡ 4 2
	◇ 5 4 3 2		◇ K 6 5 3		◇ Q J 7 6		◇ K Q 5 3 2
	♣ 7 6 3		♣ 9 8 6 4		♣ Q 9 6 2		♣ 9 8 4

5.	♠ A 8 7	6.	♠ A K 8 4	7.	♠ 7 6	8.	♠ A 7 6 2
	♡ Q 9 8		♡ 8 7 5 3		♡ Q J 7 5		♡ 2
	◇ K 7 4 3 2		◇ 4 2		◇ Q 8 7 6		◇ A J 7 5
	♣ J 2		♣ K 8 6		♣ 8 5 4		♣ 9 8 5 2

C. West 2♠ : East 2NT. West's rebid?

1.	♠ A K Q J 7	2.	♠ A K Q J 8 7 6	3.	♠ A Q 9 8 6 2
	♡ A K J 4		♡ 5 3		♡ A K
	◇ 4 3		◇ A 4		◇ A Q J
	♣ A K		♣ A K		♣ A 5

4.	♠ A K Q 8 6	5.	♠ A Q J 9 8 6 5	6.	♠ A K Q J 7
	♡ A Q 5		♡ A K Q J 8 3		♡ A
	◇ A K 7		◇ - - -		◇ 7 4
	♣ A 3		♣ - - -		♣ A K Q 6 3

D. West 2♠ : East 2NT, West rebids 3♡. What should East rebid?

1. ♠ 6 5	**2.** ♠ 9 8 7	**3.** ♠ Q 8 7	**4.** ♠ 8
♡ 4 3	♡ 7 6	♡ 4	♡ 7 2
◇ Q J 6 5	◇ Q J 7 6 3	◇ 8 7 5 3 2	◇ A J 8 6 5 3 2
♣ J 8 7 6 4	♣ 4 3 2	♣ K 9 6 5	♣ 5 3 2
5. ♠ 6 5	**6.** ♠ J 8 7	**7.** ♠ 3 2	**8.** ♠ K 8
♡ 7 6 4 3	♡ Q 5 2	♡ 9	♡ Q 9 4 3
◇ 9 6 5 2	◇ 6 5 4 2	◇ Q J 8 7 6	◇ 6 3 2
♣ 9 8 3	♣ 5 3 2	♣ Q 10 9 4 2	♣ 7 5 3 2

E. West 2♡ : East 2NT, West rebids 6◇. What should East call now?

1. ♠ J 7 6 5 4	**2.** ♠ 6 4 3 2	**3.** ♠ 8 6 5 3	**4.** ♠ 9 8 2
♡ 9 8 6	♡ 4 3	♡ 4 3	♡ A 7 6
◇ 5 4	◇ 8 7 6	◇ 5 2	◇ 4 3
♣ 6 4 2	♣ 5 4 3 2	♣ 9 8 6 3 2	♣ 7 6 5 3 2

PARTNERSHIP BIDDING PRACTICE

West is the dealer on each hand. How should the bidding go?

WEST	EAST	WEST	EAST
51.	**51.**	**54.**	**54.**
♠ A K Q 9	♠ 6 4 3	♠ 7	♠ K J 9 8 5 2
♡ Q 9	♡ J 10 8 5	♡ A K 2	♡ 3
◇ A Q J 10 8 5	◇ 4 3 2	◇ A K Q 9 8 6 4	◇ 2
♣ A	♣ K 6 3	♣ K Q	♣ 10 9 7 6 4
52.	**52.**	**55.**	**55.**
♠ Q 10 7	♠ A K 8 6 3	♠ 9 3	♠ A K Q J 5
♡ J 10 7 4	♡ K	♡ J 8 7 4	♡ A K 6 2
◇ K 8 3 2	◇ - - -	◇ 6 3	◇ A K
♣ 7 2	♣ A Q J 9 8 5 4	♣ Q 7 6 4 3	♣ K 2
53.	**53.**	**56.**	**56.**
♠ A K J 9 8 7 3	♠ 6 5 4	♠ J 5 4	♠ A 9
♡ A 6 2	♡ J 10 4	♡ 9 7	♡ A Q 3
◇ - - -	◇ Q 5 2	◇ Q 8 6 3	◇ A K 5 2
♣ A K J	♣ 8 6 3 2	♣ J 7 4 3	♣ K Q 8 6

PLAY HANDS ON SUPER-STRONG OPENINGS

Hand 17 : 2NT opening — Suit contract — Finessing

Dealer North : Nil vulnerable

NORTH
- ♠ A Q J 3
- ♡ A K
- ◇ A J 4 2
- ♣ Q J 9

WEST
- ♠ K 10 9
- ♡ 10
- ◇ 8 6 5 3
- ♣ A K 7 4 2

EAST
- ♠ 7 5 4
- ♡ 9 5 4 2
- ◇ K Q 10 9
- ♣ 10 3

SOUTH
- ♠ 8 6 2
- ♡ Q J 8 7 6 3
- ◇ 7
- ♣ 8 6 5

WEST	NORTH	EAST	SOUTH
	2NT	Pass	4♡
Pass	Pass	Pass	

Bidding : South knows N-S must have 8 or more hearts and has enough for game. Note that 3NT fails as there is no entry to the South hand.

Lead : ♣K, normal from A-K suits.

Play : East signals high-low, 10 then 3 of clubs, and ruffs the third round. The ◇ A wins the ◇ K exit and the A-K of hearts are cashed. A diamond is ruffed and the last trump is drawn. A spade is led, finessing the queen. When this finesse succeeds, another diamond is ruffed and the jack of spades is finessed. Making 10 tricks.

Hand 18 : Demand opening — Weakness response — Finessing

Dealer East : N-S vulnerable

NORTH
- ♠ 10
- ♡ J 10 9 5 3 2
- ◇ 9 8
- ♣ A 8 7 2

WEST
- ♠ A K 7 5 2
- ♡ K Q
- ◇ A K J 6
- ♣ K Q

EAST
- ♠ 8 6 4 3
- ♡ 8 7
- ◇ 5 4 3 2
- ♣ 5 4 3

SOUTH
- ♠ Q J 9
- ♡ A 6 4
- ◇ Q 10 7
- ♣ J 10 9 6

WEST	NORTH	EAST	SOUTH
		Pass	Pass
2♠	Pass	2NT	Pass
3◇	Pass	4♠	All pass

Bidding : 2NT is the negative reply. East supports the spades later.

Lead : ♡J, top of sequence.

Play : When in, West plays A-K of spades. Normally leave the last trump out, but you need to reach dummy to take the diamond finesse. Concede a spade, win the return, cash one top diamond (in case the queen drops), cross to dummy with a trump and lead a diamond, finessing the jack. The finesse for a queen is normally taken on the second round of the suit.

Hand 19 : 2NT opening — Suit response — Finessing

Dealer South : N-S vulnerable

NORTH
♠ A
♡ 8 6 5 3 2
♢ 7 4 3 2
♣ 7 5 3

WEST
♠ J 10 5 3
♡ 9 4
♢ J 10 8
♣ 10 9 8 6

EAST
♠ 9 7 4 2
♡ K 10 7
♢ 9 6 5
♣ A K Q

SOUTH
♠ K Q 8 6
♡ A Q J
♢ A K Q
♣ J 4 2

WEST	NORTH	EAST	SOUTH
			2NT
Pass	3♡	Pass	4♡
Pass	Pass	Pass	

Bidding : North's 3♡ shows *five* hearts and South has support. 3NT is beaten without difficulty as North's ♠ A entry is easily knocked out.

Lead : ♣ K, normal from A-K suits.

Play : East cashes three clubs and switches to a spade. North wins and the best chance to avoid a heart loser is to finesse for the king. Low heart, low, queen . . . the finesse works. Ruff a spade to come back to hand and lead a low heart, low, finesse the jack. The ♡ A then captures the king and declarer has the rest of the tricks.

Hand 20 : Refusing to overruff — Discarding a loser instead

Dealer West : Nil vulnerable

NORTH
♠ 8
♡ Q J 9 7 4
♢ Q 10 7 4 2
♣ 9 2

WEST
♠ 7 6
♡ 10 5 3 2
♢ 9 8 6 3
♣ Q 10 7

EAST
♠ A K Q 5 4 3 2
♡ A K
♢ A J
♣ J 8

SOUTH
♠ J 10 9
♡ 8 6
♢ K 5
♣ A K 6 5 4 3

WEST	NORTH	EAST	SOUTH
Pass	Pass	2♠	Pass
2NT	Pass	3♠	Pass
4♠	Pass	Pass	All pass

Bidding: East's 3♠ rebid shows at least 6 spades, so West raises to 4♠.

Lead: ♣ K, normal from A-K suits.

Play: North's high-low, 9 then 2, in clubs asks South to continue clubs. North ruffs the third club. If East overruffs, South's J-10-9 becomes a trump trick and with a diamond to be lost, declarer is one down. This is unlucky for East but there is a safe counter-measure. On the third club, declarer should not overruff. Discard the jack of diamonds and ten tricks are quite safe.

WEAK TWO BIDS AND 2♣ GAME FORCE

Another method of two openings which is popular, particularly among tournament players is to use 2♣ as the only super-strong opening bid. The opening bids of 2♠, 2♡ and 2♢ are then used as weak openings, like a pre-empt but with only a 6-card suit.

The 2♣ opening is artificial and forcing. Opener shows the long suit on the next round or rebids no-trumps with a balanced hand. The expectancy for the 2♣ opening is 23 HCP or more or a hand with ten playing tricks or better. Players using this approach usually adjust the range of the 2NT opening as follows :

21-22 points balanced : Open 2NT.

23-24 points balanced : Open 2♣, rebid 2NT.

25-28 points balanced : Open 2♣, rebid 3NT.

Responding to the 2♣ opening: With a poor hand (0-7 hcp), reply 2♢, the negative response. Any other reply, known as a positive response, shows 8 points or more or a particularly strong 7 hcp, such as an ace plus a king or a suit headed by A-Q-J. A positive reply commits the partnership to game and usually leads to a slam.

After 2♣ : 2♢, opener's 2NT rebid (23-24 points) is not forcing. Any other rebid by opener is forcing to game. Thus, the 2♣ opening is forcing to game except for the sequence 2♣ : 2♢, 2NT. Bidding after the 2NT rebid follows the same structure as after a 2NT opening. If responder does bid over the 2NT rebid, the partnership is going to reach game.

Weak Two Bids : These show 6-10 hcp and a strong 6-card suit. With 11 hcp and a 6-card suit, you have enough for a 1-opening. The suit should contain at least three points or at least two honors, in other words no worse than Q-J-x-x-x-x or K-10-x-x-x-x. The weak two opening in first or second seat should not contain a void or two singletons or four cards in a side major suit.

With a singleton or a void in opener's suit, it is best to pass unless you have 16 hcp or more. A change of suit is forcing and implies you do not have support for opener's suit. Opener should raise a change of suit with doubleton support or better.

With support for opener's suit, invite game with about four winners and bid game with about five winners. If you have support and six winners or more, there are good prospects for a slam. Opener has about 5-6 tricks.

PART 2

AREAS OF BIDDING COMMON TO ALL STANDARD SYSTEMS

In general, it is correct to say that when you state that you are playing a specific system, this refers only to the meaning of your bids when your side opens the bidding and the responses to those opening bids. Almost invariably, the system you play will not stipulate the methods you should use when the opponents open the bidding. Also, it is usually only the meaning of opening bids at the one-level and two-level that are dictated by system requirements. Openings at higher levels are unaffected if a standard system is being played.

There are thus several areas of bidding which are common to all standard bidding systems. This is very convenient since partners do not need to discuss their methods in these areas, as they will be using the same methods, unless they specifically agree to adopt something else. The areas which have a common treatment are :

● Slam bidding using the Blackwood Convention.

● Pre-emptive openings of 3 or more in a suit.

● Standard overcalls.

● Takeout doubles.

Each of these topics is examined in the following chapters.

CHAPTER 8
SLAM BIDDING

If you and partner have the values for a slam, it is a losing approach not to bid the slam. Even if you fail occasionally, the rewards for slams are so great that you will be in front in the long run if you succeed in more than 50% of your slams. A small slam is worthwhile with 33 points or more and a grand slam should be bid if you have at least 37 points together.

However, there is more to bidding slams than just points. It is also vital that you cannot lose the first two tricks in a small slam and that there should be little risk of a loser in a grand slam. In particular, there should not be two aces missing for a small slam, or an ace or a critical king or queen missing for a grand slam. The 33 points for a small slam need not all be high card points so that it is possible for two aces to be missing. Likewise, the 37 points for a grand slam can contain shortage points and again an ace or a key king or key queen could be missing. If you are in doubt, settle for a good small slam rather than take a risk for a grand slam.

If you know the partnership has 33 *high card* points or more, you know that there cannot be two aces missing. If you have located a good trump fit or you know that you should be in no-trumps, you can then simply bid the slam you judge to be best without further ado. For example, if partner opens 2NT and you hold 13 points with a 4-3-3-3 pattern, the commonsense bid is 6NT. You know all that you need to know to bid the slam. In other situations, you may know that there is enough strength for a slam and can tell that you cannot lose the first two tricks. For example :

♠ A Q J 8 6 4
♡ A 4
◊ 5
♣ A K 3 2

Partner passed, you opened 1♠ and partner raised to 3♠. Since partner passed initially, you can expect the jump-raise to show support and 11-12 points. Your hand is now worth 22 and so there are enough points for a small slam. As you hold three aces and a singleton in the other suit, there is no threat of losing the first two tricks. Bid 6♠.

Most of the time, however, you may know that there are enough points for a slam, but you will not be sure that there might not be two aces missing. In these situations, you will need to ask partner for aces, using the Blackwood Convention on the opposite page. With Blackwood, you are able to check on how many aces are held by the partnership and also how many kings.

Before you use Blackwood, you should be confident of two things: firstly, that there are enough points for a slam (having enough aces will not cure a deficiency in points — even all four aces will produce only four tricks, while four aces and four kings add up to eight tricks), and secondly, you know your final destination: you are aware of a strong trump fit, or you have a powerful self-sufficient trump suit, or you know no-trumps is all right.

BLACKWOOD 4NT — ASKING FOR ACES

A JUMP TO 4NT AFTER A SUIT BID ASKS PARTNER :
"HOW MANY ACES DO YOU HAVE?"
THE REPLIES ARE :

$$5\clubsuit = 0 \text{ or } 4$$
$$5\diamondsuit = 1$$
$$5\heartsuit = 2$$
$$5\spadesuit = 3$$

AFTER THE ANSWER TO 4NT, 5NT ASKS PARTNER :
"HOW MANY KINGS DO YOU HOLD?"
THE REPLIES ARE :

$$6\clubsuit = 0$$
$$6\diamondsuit = 1$$
$$6\heartsuit = 2$$
$$6\spadesuit = 3$$
$$6NT = 4$$

In order to use the 5NT ask for kings, you should have ambitions for a grand slam. The partnership should have the values for a grand slam, a strong trump suit and there should not be any aces missing. In other words, the use of 5NT asking for kings promises that the partnership holds all the aces.

The 4NT bid is usually Blackwood asking for aces, but if 4NT is used as an immediate response to an opening bid of no-trumps (e.g. 1NT: 4NT *or* 2NT: 4NT) this is not used as Blackwood but as an invitation to 6NT. Opener is asked to pass with a minimum opening and to bid on with more than minimum points. If you wish to check on aces after a no-trump opening, you will have to bid a suit first (e.g. 1NT: 3♡ or 2NT: 3◇) and then bid 4NT later. It is an ask for aces if there has been a suit bid in the auction.

EXERCISES ON SLAM BIDDING

A. In each of the following auctions you are South with the hand shown. Would you say that you are in the slam zone or the game zone?

1. ♠ K 10 9 6 4
   ♡ K J 5
   ◇ A 9 7 3
   ♣ 4

N	S
2NT	?

2. ♠ K 6 3
   ♡ K 9
   ◇ K 10 7 6 5 3
   ♣ A 2

N	S
2♡	?

3. ♠ K Q 7
   ♡ K J 4 3
   ◇ A 8 7
   ♣ J 4 3

N	S
1NT	?

4. ♠ A K J
   ♡ K Q 10 9 7 6
   ◇ K Q
   ♣ J 6

N	S
	1♡
4♡	?

5. ♠ Q 5
   ♡ A Q 8 4 3
   ◇ K 7 2
   ♣ Q 4 3

N	S
	1♡
3♡	?

6. ♠ 6
   ♡ K 9
   ◇ A 4 3 2
   ♣ A K Q 7 6 2

N	S
1♡	2♣
3♡	?

B. In each of the following auctions you are South with the hand shown. What is your next call in each of the auctions?

1. ♠ A J 8 3
   ♡ A 6
   ◇ A Q J 4 2
   ♣ 8 3

N	S
	1◇
1♠	3♠
4NT	?

2. ♠ A 8 7
   ♡ A 4
   ◇ A J 9 4
   ♣ A 7 4 3

N	S
	1NT
3♡	3NT
4NT	?

3. ♠ K Q 7
   ♡ K Q J 4 3
   ◇ 7
   ♣ A Q 4 3

N	S
	1♡
3♡	4NT
5◇	?

4. ♠ J 4 3 2
   ♡ K 8 5
   ◇ 3
   ♣ A K J 6 4

N	S
1♡	2♣
2◇	3♡
4NT	1?

5. ♠ K 8 4 2
   ♡ A 9
   ◇ Q J 9 8
   ♣ K 8 6

N	S
1♡	2NT
4NT	5◇
5♡	?

6. ♠ K Q 3
   ♡ 6 4 2
   ◇ A K 5 2
   ♣ A J 8

N	S
1♡	3NT
4NT	5♡
5NT	?

C. You hold :   What is your next call in each of these auctions?

♠ K Q 8 5 3	**a.** You	Ptnr.	**b.** You	Ptnr.	**c.** You	Ptnr.
♡ A Q J 2	**1♠**	**3♠**	**1♠**	**3♠**	**1♠**	**3♠**
◇ K Q 4	**4NT**	**5♡**	**4NT**	**5♠**	**4NT**	**5♠**
♣ 6	**?**		**5NT**	**6◇**	**5NT**	**6♡**
			?		**?**	

D. You hold :   What is your next call in each of these auctions?

♠ A 9 5	**a.** You	Ptnr.	**b.** You	Ptnr.	**c.** You	Ptnr.
♡ A J 6 3 2	**1♡**	**4NT**			**1♠**	**1♡**
◇ - - -	**5♡**	**6◇**	**1♠**	**1♡**	**1♠**	
♣ Q J 8 7 6	**?**		**2♡**	**4NT**	**2♣**	**4NT**
			5♡	**6◇**	**5♡**	**5♠**
			?		**?**	

E. You hold :   What is your next call in each of these auctions?

♠ A 8 4 3 2	**a.** You	Ptnr.	**b.** You	Ptnr.	**c.** You	Ptnr.
♡ K Q 10	**1♠**	**2♣**	**1♠**	**2◇**	**1♠**	**2♡**
◇ 6	**4♣**	**4NT**	**3♣**	**5♠**	**4♡**	**5♡**
♣ K Q J 3	**5◇**	**5♡**	**?**		**?**	
	?					

PARTNERSHIP BIDDING PRACTICE

West is the dealer on each hand. How should the bidding go?

WEST	EAST	WEST	EAST
57.	**57.**	**60.**	**60.**
♠ A K J 7 4	♠ 10 3	♠ A Q J 7 6	♠ 9 5
♡ A K Q 3	♡ J 8	♡ A Q J 5	♡ K 7 4 3
◇ A J	◇ K Q 6 2	◇ K 3	◇ A Q 7
♣ J 3	♣ K Q 9 7 4	♣ K 9	♣ A J 5 4
58.	**58.**	**61.**	**61.**
♠ A Q 8	♠ K 6 4	♠ K 9 8	♠ A Q 6
♡ K Q 9 7	♡ A J 2	♡ Q J 7	♡ A K 3
◇ A K 3	◇ 8 7 4 2	◇ A Q J	◇ K 8 5 2
♣ 8 7 2	♣ A K Q	♣ A K Q 6	♣ 9 5 4
59.	**59.**	**62.**	**62.**
♠ K 6	♠ A Q J	♠ A J	♠ K 9 4
♡ 9 5 3 2	♡ A K Q 8 7 6	♡ A K Q J 8 4	♡ 5 3 2
◇ K 7 4	◇ A Q 3	◇ A K Q 2	◇ 8 7 5
♣ A 8 4 2	♣ K	♣ A	♣ K 8 6 2

PLAY HANDS ON SLAM BIDDING

Hand 21 : 2NT opening — Setting up extra tricks — Finessing

Dealer North : Nil vulnerable

NORTH
- ♠ 9 6 5 2
- ♡ J 10 9 4 3
- ◇ 6 5 2
- ♣ 10

WEST
- ♠ Q J 4
- ♡ K Q 6
- ◇ K 7 4
- ♣ J 8 3 2

EAST
- ♠ A K 7
- ♡ A 8 2
- ◇ A Q 3
- ♣ K Q 5 4

SOUTH
- ♠ 10 8 3
- ♡ 7 5
- ◇ J 10 9 8
- ♣ A 9 7 6

WEST	NORTH	EAST	SOUTH
	Pass	2NT	Pass
6NT	Pass	Pass	Pass

Bidding : With 12 points opposite 22 at least, West has enough for slam.

Lead : ◇ J, top of sequence.

Play : With 9 tricks outside clubs, 3 club tricks are needed to succeed. Win the lead and play the ♣ K. If it wins, continue with the ♣ Q, while if the ♣ K is taken by the ace, win the return and cash the ♣ Q. When North shows out on the second club, take a finesse of dummy's 8 next time.

Wrong play: Playing winners in the other suits before tackling clubs. Failing to take the club finesse.

Hand 22 : Leaving the top trump out while you discard a loser

Dealer East : N-S vulnerable

NORTH
- ♠ J 6
- ♡ 9 7 5 3 2
- ◇ A 2
- ♣ A Q J 5

WEST
- ♠ 9 8 7 5 4 3
- ♡ 10
- ◇ 10 9 3
- ♣ 10 4 3

EAST
- ♠ K Q 10
- ♡ Q J 8
- ◇ 8 4
- ♣ K 9 7 6 2

SOUTH
- ♠ A 2
- ♡ A K 6 4
- ◇ K Q J 7 6 5
- ♣ 8

WEST	NORTH	EAST	SOUTH
		Pass	1◇
Pass	1♡	Pass	4♡
Pass	4NT	Pass	5♡
Pass	6♡	All pass	

Bidding : 4♡ showed enough for game opposite 6 points, so that South must have 19-20 points or more. North, with 14 points in all, bids to a slam after checking on aces.

Lead: ♠ K. In a trump contract, the lead from a K-Q suit is the king.

Play : Win the ♠ A. Play the A-K of hearts, the ◇ A, a diamond to the king and on the third diamond, pitch your spade loser. East ruffs, but the spade loser has been eliminated.

Hand 23 : Rejecting a finesse — Delaying trumps — Discarding a loser

Dealer South : Both vulnerable

NORTH
♠ A K Q J 2
♡ K Q J 4
◇ A Q J
♣ 2

WEST
♠ 10 8
♡ 6
◇ 10 9 8 7 5 4
♣ Q 10 8 7

EAST
♠ 9 6 5 4 3
♡ A 8
◇ K 2
♣ 9 6 5 4

SOUTH
♠ 7
♡ 10 9 7 5 3 2
◇ 6 3
♣ A K J 3

WEST	NORTH	EAST	SOUTH
			Pass
Pass	2♠	Pass	3♡
Pass	4NT	Pass	5◇
Pass	6♡	All pass	

Bidding : South's 3♡, a positive reply, is enough for North to check on aces and bid the slam.

Lead : ◇ 10. Top of sequence.

Play : Win the ◇ A, play ♠ A-K to discard the diamond loser and then lead trumps. Later the last trump is drawn and losing clubs are ruffed or discarded on the spade winners.

Wrong play : (1) The unnecessary diamond finesse at trick 1.
(2) Playing trumps before taking a discard. East wins ♡ A, cashes ◇ K.

Hand 24 : Card combinations — Setting up winners to discard losers

Dealer West : Nil vulnerable

NORTH
♠ Q 10 9
♡ J 10 9 8
◇ Q 10 9
♣ 9 6 5

WEST
♠ K 8 6 5 4 2
♡ A
◇ A K 5 4
♣ K 8

EAST
♠ A J 7 3
♡ K Q
◇ 8 7 3
♣ Q J 10 4

SOUTH
♠ - - -
♡ 7 6 5 4 3 2
◇ J 6 2
♣ A 7 3 2

WEST	NORTH	EAST	SOUTH
1♠	Pass	3♠	Pass
4NT	Pass	5◇	Pass
6♠	Pass	Pass	Pass

Bidding : After East's 3♠, showing support and 13 points or more, West revalues to 21 points, checks on aces and bids the small slam.

Lead : ♡ J, top of sequence.

Play : Win the ♡ A, play the ♠ K next, preserving the A-J tenace in dummy in case a finesse becomes necessary. When South shows out, finesse the ♠ J, cash the ♠ A to draw the last trump and then lead a club to the king and continue clubs. Later you can discard two diamond losers on dummy's winners.

CHAPTER 9
PRE-EMPTIVE OPENING BIDS

Without interference, most pairs with a little experience can bid well enough to the best spot most of the time. Information is exchanged by the partnership's dialogue. For example, 1♡ : 2♣, 2◊ : 2♡, 4♡ can be translated into: 'I have hearts.' : 'What about clubs?', 'No, I have diamonds, too.' : 'Oh, I prefer your hearts.', 'All right, let's try 4♡ then.'

Imagine that before any of the above dialogue took place, you had made a 3♠ opening. What happens to their dialogue? Opening bids of 3-in-a-suit, 4-in-a-suit or 5♣ or 5◊ openings are called pre-empts because by getting in first, you aim *to shut out* the opponents. Pre-empts force the opposition into *guessing* what to do. Their decisions have to be made without any clear knowledge of what is held by their partner. When they have to guess at the contract, they will sometimes make the wrong guess. That is your profit.

A pre-emptive bid is made on the first round of bidding. There is no such concept as a pre-emptive *rebid*, since if the opponents have not been in the bidding on the first round, there is no need to shut them out A pre-empt can be made in any position, by opener, by responder or by either defender. Pre-empts are more effective the sooner they are made since that reduces the amount of information the opponents can exchange. Therefore, pre-empt as high as you dare as early as possible. Once you have pre-empted, do not bid again unless your partner makes a forcing bid.

A pre-emptive bid skips two or more levels of bidding. For example, an opening bid of 3◊ is a pre-empt because it skips over 1◊ and 2◊. Likewise, 1♣ : 3◊ is a pre-empt because it skips over 1◊ and 2◊. However, 1♠ : 3◊ would not be a pre-empt, as it skips over only one level, the 2◊ bid. The 3◊ response here is a jump-shift, the most powerful response possible.

The normal pre-emptive opening contains :

● **6-10 high card points, and**

● **A strong 7-card or longer suit**

A pre-emptive opening may have fewer than 6 points if it contains the right number of playing tricks (see opposite), but in practice, this is very rare. It may also be a very powerful 6-card suit rather than a 7-card suit, but this is rare, too. Do not pre-empt if you have a 4-card or longer major as a second suit.

When you have a hand suitable for a pre-empt, you may open with a bid of 3 or a bid of 4 (and if your suit is a minor, you may even begin with a bid of 5♣ or 5◇). How can you judge whether you should open with a 3-bid or with a higher bid? The answer depends on the number of playing tricks you hold. The Rule of 3 and 2 states that you should count your playing tricks and add 3 tricks if not vulnerable, or 2 tricks if vulnerable, and make the opening bid appropriate to this total number of tricks. In other words :

With 6 playing tricks, open 3 if not vulnerable, pass if vulnerable.

With 7 playing tricks, open 4 if not vulnerable, open 3 if vulnerable.

With 8 playing tricks and not vulnerable: open 4 if your suit is a major, but open 5 if your suit is a minor. If vulnerable, open 4 in either case.

With 9 playing tricks, open 4 if your suit is a major and 5 if it is a minor.

HOW TO COUNT YOUR PLAYING TRICKS :

1. Count every card after the third card in a suit as one playing trick.

2. In the top three cards of each suit, count each ace and each king as one trick.

3. Count each queen as one trick if there is a second honor card in that suit.

4. Count no tricks for a singleton king, singleton queen or queen doubleton. Count only one trick for holding K-Q doubleton.

RESPONDING TO PARTNER'S PRE-EMPTIVE OPENING :

1. Assess how many tricks your partner's opening has shown by deducting three if your side is not vulnerable or two if your side is vulnerable.

2. Add to this your own 'quick tricks' : Count the A, K or Q of partner's suit as one trick each. In other suits, count A-K as 2, A-Q as 1½, A as 1, K-Q as 1, and K as ½. If you have support for opener's suit, count an outside singleton as one and an outside void as two.

3. If the total is less than partner's bid or just enough for the contract, pass.

4. If the total is more than partner's bid, you should bid on to game (but if partner's bid is already a game, you would pass). If the total is 12 or more, bid on to a slam, provided that you are not missing two aces.

5. Over an opening bid of 3♣ or 3◇, you may try 3NT with a strong balanced hand and at least one stopper in each of the outside suits.

6. Over other opening pre-empts, prefer to stick with partner's suit unless you have a strong hand and a long, powerful suit of your own. A change-of-suit in response to a pre-empt is forcing.

7. Do not 'rescue' partner from a pre-empt. With a weak hand, pass.

EXERCISES ON PRE-EMPTIVE BIDDING

A. Pre-empts are based on playing trick potential. How many tricks would you expect to win with each of these suits as trumps?

1. A K Q x x x x x   **7.** A Q x x x x x   **13.** K J x x x x x x

2. A K Q x x x x   **8.** A K x x x x x   **14.** K x x x x x x

3. A K Q x x x   **9.** A J x x x x   **15.** Q J 10 x x x x

4. A K J x x x x x   **10.** A x x x x x x   **16.** Q x x x x x x x

5. A K J x x x x   **11.** K Q J x x x x   **17.** J x x x x x x

6. A Q J x x x x   **12.** K Q x x x x x x   **18.** x x x x x x x x x

B. You are dealer. What action do you take with these hands if you are (i) not vulnerable?   (ii) vulnerable?

1. ♠ Q J 10 8 7 4 2
   ♡ 5
   ◇ K Q J
   ♣ 5 4

2. ♠ 8
   ♡ K Q J 9 7 6 5 4
   ◇ 4 3
   ♣ 3 2

3. ♠ K 3
   ♡ 5 4
   ◇ 8 7
   ♣ A K J 9 8 6 2

4. ♠ 3 2
   ♡ - - -
   ◇ A K Q 9 8 7 5 4 2
   ♣ 5 2

5. ♠ K J 10 7 6 5 4
   ♡ 6
   ◇ Q J 10 9 6
   ♣ - - -

6. ♠ 5
   ♡ 4 3
   ◇ 7 4 3 2
   ♣ A K Q 7 6 4

7. ♠ K Q J 8 7
   ♡ 5
   ◇ Q J 10 6
   ♣ 4 3 2

8. ♠ K 6 3 2
   ♡ 9
   ◇ 3
   ♣ A 8 7 6 4 3 2

9. ♠ J 9 8 6 5 4
   ♡ A K 3
   ◇ 9 8 7
   ♣ 3

10. ♠ A K 8 7 6 4
   ♡ Q 9 7 6 3
   ◇ 2
   ♣ 6

11. ♠ A 5
   ♡ A K Q 9 7 6 3
   ◇ Q 9 7
   ♣ 2

12. ♠ 6 5
   ♡ A K Q 9 7 6 3
   ◇ 9 7 3
   ♣ 2

13. ♠ 4
   ♡ J 9 7 6 4 3 2
   ◇ A 2
   ♣ J 8 6

14. ♠ A K Q J 5 3 2
   ♡ A K
   ◇ Q 9 7
   ♣ A

15. ♠ K Q J 6 5 3 2
   ♡ 4
   ◇ 2
   ♣ Q 10 7 3

C. Partner opens Three Hearts. What is your response if you are
(i) not vulnerable?   (ii) vulnerable?

1. ♠ A J 9 8 7
   ♡ 5 3
   ◊ Q J 7 6
   ♣ 8 5

2. ♠ A J 9 8 6 4
   ♡ 3
   ◊ Q J 7
   ♣ 6 5 2

3. ♠ A K 5 4 3
   ♡ - - -
   ◊ J 8 7 4 3
   ♣ 9 7 6

4. ♠ A K J 8 7 2
   ♡ 5
   ◊ A Q J
   ♣ J 3 2

5. ♠ A 8 7
   ♡ Q 7 6 5
   ◊ K 8 3
   ♣ 6 4 2

6. ♠ 7
   ♡ Q 4 3
   ◊ A K 8 4 3
   ♣ J 6 3 2

7. ♠ A Q J
   ♡ 5 4 3
   ◊ Q J 10 6
   ♣ K Q 10

8. ♠ A K 6 5 3 2
   ♡ 4 3
   ◊ A 7
   ♣ Q J 7

9. ♠ A K J 4 3
   ♡ 9 7
   ◊ K Q J 7 6
   ♣ 2

10. ♠ K 8 7 6 4
    ♡ 3
    ◊ A J 7 6 5 2
    ♣ 4

11. ♠ A 5
    ♡ K 7 6 4
    ◊ A 9 7
    ♣ A K Q J

12. ♠ A 6 5
    ♡ K 9 4
    ◊ A K Q 8 7 2
    ♣ 5

PARTNERSHIP BIDDING PRACTICE

West is the dealer, neither side vulnerable. How should the bidding go?

WEST	EAST	WEST	EAST
63.	**63.**	**66.**	**66.**
♠ K Q J 8 6 4 3	♠ 10 2	♠ A 7 6	♠ 4
♡ 8 4	♡ A K 6	♡ 7	♡ K Q J 8 6 5 2
◊ 4 3	◊ A K 7 5	◊ A J 8 4 3	◊ 9 6
♣ 9 7	♣ 8 6 5 4	♣ 6 5 4 2	♣ 8 7 3
64.	**64.**	**67.**	**67.**
♠ 8	♠ A Q 3	♠ A Q J 9 6 4 3 2	♠ K 8 7
♡ 10 6	♡ A J 7 2	♡ 9 4	♡ 7
◊ A Q J 7 6 5 4	◊ 8 3 2	◊ 8	◊ A K 4 3
♣ 7 6 2	♣ A J 10	♣ 9 7	♣ A 8 6 4 3
65.	**65.**	**68.**	**68.**
♠ 9 3	♠ A K 7 6 5 4	♠ 8 2	♠ A K Q
♡ 8	♡ A 9 5	♡ A 4	♡ K Q J 7 5 3 2
◊ A K J 7 5 3 2	◊ 8	◊ K Q 9 7 4 3 2	◊ 6
♣ 9 5 3	♣ A Q 4	♣ 7 5	♣ A Q

PLAY HANDS ON PRE-EMPTIVE OPENINGS

Hand 25 : Shut-out opening — Establishing a second suit in hand

Dealer North : Nil vulnerable

NORTH
♠ A K Q 9 7 6 5
♡ 2
◇ 8
♣ 9 8 7 3

WEST
♠ J 8 3
♡ 10 9 6 5 4
◇ K Q 10
♣ A K

EAST
♠ 10
♡ K Q J 8 3
◇ A J 5
♣ 6 5 4 2

SOUTH
♠ 4 2
♡ A 7
◇ 9 7 6 4 3 2
♣ Q J 10

WEST	NORTH	EAST	SOUTH
	4♠	All pass	

Bidding: With 7 tricks not vulnerable, North has enough to open 4♠ rather than 3♠. Neither East nor West are strong enough to bid over that. Note that if West were the dealer, West would open 1♡ and, over North's 4♠ overcall, East would compete to 5♡ which would succeed. North's 4♠ opening has shut East-West out of the game they could make.

Lead : ♡ K, top of sequence.

Play: Win ♡ A, draw trumps in three rounds and then lead clubs at each opportunity to set up two extra tricks after the ♣ A-K are forced out.

Hand 26 : Play from dummy at trick 1 — Establishing a long suit

Dealer East : N-S vulnerable

NORTH
♠ K Q 7 6
♡ K 10 8 7 3
◇ J 9 8
♣ 2

WEST
♠ A 10 9 3
♡ A 6 5
◇ A K 10
♣ 9 5 4

EAST
♠ 4 2
♡ Q 4
◇ 6 3
♣ K Q J 8 7 6 3

SOUTH
♠ J 8 5
♡ J 9 2
◇ Q 7 5 4 2
♣ A 10

WEST	NORTH	EAST	SOUTH
		3♣	Pass
3NT	Pass	Pass	Pass

Bidding: With 6 playing tricks and not vulnerable, East may open 3♣. With a balanced hand, all outside suits covered and four tricks opposite East's six, West should choose 3NT.

Lead : ♡7. Fourth-highest.

Play: Play the ♡ Q from dummy, hoping to win the trick (when North has the king). When the ♡ Q holds, lead clubs to force out the ace. Once the ♣ A has gone, dummy's clubs are high. South should return a heart, partner's suit, but West wins and cashes the clubs and other winners.

Hand 27 : Slam bidding after a pre-empt — Setting up a long suit

Dealer South : Both vulnerable

WEST	NORTH	EAST	SOUTH
			4◇
Pass	4NT	Pass	5◇
Pass	6◇	All pass	

NORTH
- ♠ J
- ♡ A Q J
- ◇ K 10 9
- ♣ A 9 8 7 6 3

15

WEST	EAST
♠ K 10 9 5 4 3	♠ A Q 7 6 2
♡ 9 8 6	♡ K 5 4 3 2
◇ - - -	◇ 7
♣ K Q J 4	♣ 10 2

SOUTH
- ♠ 8
- ♡ 10 7
- ◇ A Q J 8 6 5 4 3 2
- ♣ 5

4D

Bidding : With 8 tricks vulnerable, South opens 4◇ rather than 3◇. With 3 sure winners and potential for another in three other suits, North bids to slam after checking on aces.

Lead : ♣K. Top of sequence.

Play : The best play is to set up the club suit. Win ♣A, ruff a club high, diamond to dummy's 9, ruff a club, diamond to dummy's 10, ruff a club. The last two clubs in dummy are high. Diamond to the king (or a heart to the ace) and play the clubs on which a spade and a heart are discarded.

Hand 28 : Pre-emptive opening — Counting tricks — Slam bidding

Dealer West : Nil vulnerable

WEST	NORTH	EAST	SOUTH
3♡	Pass	4NT	Pass
5◇	Pass	7NT	All pass

NORTH
- ♠ 10 6 4 3 2
- ♡ - - -
- ◇ K 9 3 2
- ♣ 10 8 7 6

WEST	EAST
♠ 7	♠ A 9 5
♡ A 9 8 7 6 3 2	♡ K 10 5 4
◇ Q J 10	◇ A 6
♣ 4 3	♣ A K Q J

SOUTH
- ♠ K Q J 8
- ♡ Q J
- ◇ 8 7 5 4
- ♣ 9 5 2

Bidding : With five playing tricks in hearts and one in diamonds, West opens 3♡ not vulnerable. East has enough for a slam and after finding the missing ace, East counts tricks : 1 in spades, 7 in hearts (given that West has seven hearts to the ace), 1 in diamonds and 4 in clubs. With 13 top winners, choose 7NT, mainly because you eliminate the risk of the opening lead being ruffed.

Lead : ♠K. Top of sequence.

Play : Win and play out the hearts, being careful to play the ♡10 early so that the hearts are not 'blocked'.

CHAPTER 10
STANDARD OVERCALLS

With normal luck, your side will open the bidding only half the time. This chapter and the next are concerned with the actions you may take after the bidding has been opened by the other side. There is only one opening bid in each auction, the first bid made, and there is only one opening bidder. The partner of the opening bidder is the responder and the opposing side is known as 'the defenders' and their bidding is called 'defensive bidding'. A bid made by a defender is an 'overcall' (or an 'interpose') but not an opening. There is no such concept as 'opening for your side' after the other side has made a bid. The principles for defensive bidding are not the same as for opening the bidding and it is essential to appreciate the differences.

THE 1NT OVERCALL shows—

A balanced hand, 16-18 points and at least one stopper in their suit.

The minimum holdings which qualify as a stopper are the ace, K-x, Q-x-x or J-x-x-x, i.e. a holding where if they lead their suit from the top, you will win a trick in that suit. Bidding after the 1NT overcall follows the same structure as after an opening bid of 1NT.

THE SUIT OVERCALL :

The great difference between opening the bidding (constructive bidding) and bidding after the opponents have opened (defensive bidding) is this : With 13 points or more, you would always *open* the bidding, yet if they have already opened the bidding, you should pass *unless your hand fits the requirements for an overcall or for a takeout double* (see next chapter). Thus, if they have opened, there is no obligation for you to bid, even if you have 13 points or 15 points or 17 points... The most common strong hands on which you would pass are balanced hands up to 15 points (too weak for the 1NT overcall) if they are not suitable for a takeout double, and those hands which have length and strength in a suit bid by the opponents.

While there are no suit quality requirements for *opening* and while you might *open* in a very weak suit, overcalls in a suit are based on strongish suits at least five cards long. The essence of the overcall is the long, strong suit. If your suit is strong, make an overcall even with as few as 8 or 9 HCP.

A suit overcall at the 1-level shows :
- A strong suit, at least five cards long, and
- 8-15 high card points

A suit overcall at the 2-level (not a jump-overcall) shows :
- A strong suit, at least five cards long, and
- 10-15 high card points

Thus, you can see that an overcall might be as strong as a minimum opening hand, but it need not be that strong, and can be quite weak in high cards. Just how good must a suit be to qualify as a 'strong suit'? An excellent guide for overcalls and for pre-emptive openings is the **SUIT QUALITY TEST** :

Count the number of cards in the suit you wish to bid. Add the number of honor cards in that suit (but count the jack or ten as a full honor only if the suit also contains at least one higher honor).

The total is the number of tricks for which you may bid that suit. Thus, if the total is 7, you may bid your suit at the 1-level. If the total is 8, you may bid your suit at the 1-level or the 2-level if necessary. If the total is 9, you may bid your suit at the 1-level, the 2-level or, if necessary, the 3-level.

RESPONDING TO A SUIT OVERCALL :

Below 8 points, you should normally pass, unless you have good support for partner. With exactly 8 points, bid if you have something worthwhile to say, otherwise pass. With 9 or more points, you should find some bid. Raising partner shows 8-11 points (but only three trumps are required), a jump-raise would show 12-15 and a raise from the 1-level to game would be based on 16 points or more. With their suit stopped, you may reply 1NT (8-11 points), 2NT (12-15) or 3NT (16-18). A change of suit at the 1-level would show 8-15 points and a good 5-card suit, while at the 2-level it would show 10-15 points plus the good 5-card or longer suit.

None of the preceding actions is forcing. To force the overcaller to bid again, you must jump-shift (jump in a new suit to show 16 or more points and a good 5-card or longer suit) or bid the enemy suit (an artificial forcing bid, called a 'cue bid').

After partner has replied to your overcall, you may pass with a minimum overcall if you have nothing worthwhile to add, but keep bidding if—
(a) Partner's reply was forcing, *or*
(b) You have more than a minimum overcall (e.g. in the 13-15 point zone), *or*
(c) You are minimum but you have something extra worth showing.

THE JUMP-OVERCALL :

A jump-overcall is an overcall of one more than the minimum required, for example, (1♣) : 2♡ or (1♢) : 3♣. The jump-overcall shows a good six-card or longer suit and 16 points or more, usually 16-19 points. This method is known as strong jump-overcalls. (Other methods which are in use are weak jump-overcalls — 6-10 HCP and a six-card or longer suit — and intermediate jump-overcalls — 12-15 HCP and a six-card or longer suit.) You may assume that you are using strong jump-overcalls unless you and your partner have specifically agreed to use one of the other methods.

One-suited hands are normally shown simply by bidding your long suit. However, hands with a good five-card suit but which are too strong for a simple overcall are shown by a double first, followed by a bid of your long suit on the next round (see next chapter).

RESPONDING TO A STRONG JUMP-OVERCALL :

You should respond to a strong jump-overcall with 6 points or more.

If partner's suit is a major, your first priority would be to raise that major. Only two trumps are required to raise a jump-overcall, since the suit will be at least six cards long. With 10 points or more, you could raise a major suit jump-overcall from the 2-level to the 4-level. Without support, you would bid the other major with at least five cards there, or bid no-trumps if you have their suit stopped. Your last choice would be to introduce a minor suit, but if there is nothing else available, bid a long minor.

If partner's suit is a minor, bid a long major as first priority, no-trumps as your second choice and raise the minor if neither of these actions is available. A change of suit in reply to a jump-overcall is forcing. With a strong hand in reply to an overcall and no clearcut action, you may force partner to keep bidding if you bid the enemy suit, an artificial forcing action.

DOUBLE AND TRIPLE JUMP-OVERCALLS :

A double or triple jump-overcall, such as (1♣) : 3♠ or (1♢) : 4♡, is a pre-empt since it skips over two or more levels of bidding. Pre-emptive jump-overcalls follow the same rules as a pre-emptive opening bid. The suit should have at least seven cards and it should be a strong suit, conforming to the **Suit Quality Test**. The Rule of 3 and 2 applies and the normal high card strength is 6-10 points. However, pre-emptive overcalls of 4♡ or 4♠ are more flexible and the strength can be up to 15 HCP (since your bid is already game and slam is unlikely after they have opened the bidding).

EXERCISES ON OVERCALLS

A. Your right-hand opponent opens 1◊. Do you bid or pass on the following hands? If you decide to bid, what bid do you make?

1.	♠ KJ42	2.	♠ A9	3.	♠ AQ9	4.	♠ KQ
	♡ A7		♡ KQ83		♡ KQ83		♡ 9432
	◊ Q52		◊ AJ7		◊ 74		◊ AKJ97
	♣ KJ64		♣ QJ82		♣ AQ53		♣ J2

B. Your right-hand opponent opens 1♣. What action do you take?

1.	♠ KQ9743	2.	♠ KQJ76	3.	♠ KQ97
	♡ 764		♡ 7		♡ 3
	◊ K82		◊ A542		◊ A872
	♣ 6		♣ 765		♣ Q763

4.	♠ 7	5.	♠ A	6.	♠ AQJ10754
	♡ AJ72		♡ AJ72		♡ 6
	◊ AQJ93		◊ J8532		◊ Q953
	♣ 763		♣ Q97		♣ 7

7.	♠ AQ942	8.	♠ AQ	9.	♠ AQ
	♡ 7		♡ AKJ754		♡ 97532
	◊ AKJ53		◊ Q43		◊ KQ
	♣ 62		♣ 62		♣ Q872

C. Your right-hand opponent opens 1♠. What action do you take?

1.	♠ K7	2.	♠ K7	3.	♠ 76
	♡ 64		♡ AQ		♡ K4
	◊ AQJ732		◊ Q8632		◊ A54
	♣ 763		♣ Q986		♣ AKQJ75

4.	♠ AQ	5.	♠ 7	6.	♠ AK1074
	♡ 853		♡ A109862		♡ K
	◊ A5		◊ AKJ2		◊ Q97
	♣ AKQJ43		♣ 83		♣ J863

7.	♠ ---	8.	♠ ---	9.	♠ J864
	♡ 76		♡ 764		♡ 62
	◊ KQJ98643		◊ KQJ965		◊ Q7
	♣ AJ10		♣ K962		♣ AK842

D. **N   E   S   W**   The bidding has started as on the left.
     1◇   No   1♡   ?   What action should West take on these hands?

1. ♠ A J 7 4   **2.** ♠ K Q J 8 4   **3.** ♠ Q J 10 9 7 4 3
     ♡ J 5 2   ♡ A Q   ♡ 6
     ◇ K Q 5 2   ◇ 5 4 3 2   ◇ - - -
     ♣ A 7   ♣ 7 6   ♣ A 8 4 3 2

E. **N   E   S   W**   The bidding has started as on the left.
     1♠   No   2♣   ?   What action should West take on these hands?

1. ♠ K 6 3 2   **2.** ♠ 6   **3.** ♠ A Q 9 7
     ♡ Q J 8 2   ♡ K Q J 10 9 4 3   ♡ A 4 3
     ◇ A K 7   ◇ K Q 3   ◇ 9 2
     ♣ K Q   ♣ A Q   ♣ K Q J 5

F. **N   E   S   W**   The bidding has started as on the left.
     1♣   1♡   No   ?   What action should West take on these hands?

1. ♠ K 8 4 3   **2.** ♠ 6   **3.** ♠ 6 4
     ♡ 7 6   ♡ K 8 4 3 2   ♡ K 8 4 3
     ◇ K 7 6 3   ◇ A K 8 6 5   ◇ A 8 5 4 2
     ♣ 9 4 3   ♣ 7 4   ♣ 7 2

4. ♠ Q 6   **5.** ♠ A 6 5   **6.** ♠ A 9 7
     ♡ K 8 4   ♡ 3   ♡ 7 6
     ◇ A K 8 5 3   ◇ K Q J 6 4 2   ◇ K 10 8 6
     ♣ 7 5 2   ♣ 7 6 3   ♣ Q J 9 4

7. ♠ A J 8   **8.** ♠ A Q 9 7 4 3   **9.** ♠ A Q 8
     ♡ Q 4 3   ♡ 7 2   ♡ K 7
     ◇ J 10 7 4   ◇ K 8 4   ◇ Q J 10 7
     ♣ K Q 10   ♣ 6 3   ♣ K Q 8 6

G. **N   E   S   W**   East's 2♠ is a strong jump-overcall.
     1♡   2♠   No   ?   What action should West take on these hands?

1. ♠ 10 7 6   **2.** ♠ K 7 4 2   **3.** ♠ 7 6
     ♡ Q 9   ♡ 4   ♡ K Q 10
     ◇ A 8 7 4 2   ◇ Q J 9 5   ◇ 8 7 6 4 2
     ♣ 5 4 3   ♣ 8 7 5 2   ♣ Q 10 3

PARTNERSHIP BIDDING PRACTICE
FEATURING OVERCALLS

There is no North-South bidding other than that shown.

WEST	EAST	WEST	EAST
69.	**69.**	**74.**	**74.**
S. opens 1♣.	S. opens 1♣.	N. opens 1♡.	N. opens 1♡.
♠ A J 8	♠ K Q 3	♠ A J	♠ K Q 9 7 6 2
♡ K Q 9 8 6 3	♡ 7 5	♡ 7 5 4 2	♡ 9 3
◇ 7 6 2	◇ J 9 8 3	◇ K Q 3	◇ A 8
♣ 8	♣ A 9 7 4	♣ 8 6 4 2	♣ A K 5
70.	**70.**	**75.**	**75.**
S. opens 1♣.	S. opens 1♣.	N. opens 1♡.	N. opens 1♡.
♠ A Q 7	♠ K J	♠ Q J 7 6 4	♠ A 9 3
♡ K Q	♡ J 10 9 7 4 2	♡ 7	♡ 6 2
◇ A 9 8 3	◇ K Q 6 2	◇ Q 9 3	◇ A K J 8 7 4
♣ Q 8 7 2	♣ 3	♣ A J 8 6	♣ 9 3
71.	**71.**	**76.**	**76.**
N. opens 1◇.	N. opens 1◇.	S. opens 1♠.	S. opens 1♠.
♠ A 7 6	♠ K 8 3	♠ 7 5	♠ K 8 4 2
♡ K Q 3	♡ A J 10 7 6 4	♡ A 8 3	♡ K 9 7
◇ J 8 7 4	◇ A Q	◇ 7 6	◇ A J 5 2
♣ 7 3 2	♣ Q 4	♣ A K J 9 3 2	♣ Q 8
72.	**72.**	**77.**	**77.**
N. opens 1◇.	N. opens 1◇.	S. opens 1♠.	S. opens 1♠.
♠ K Q J	♠ A 7 4	♠ 6 4 3 2	♠ 9
♡ 9 8 5 2	♡ K Q J 7 3	♡ A 8	♡ K Q J 7 5 4
◇ Q 3	◇ K 8 4	◇ K Q 7	◇ A 6 3
♣ A J 8 5	♣ 7 3	♣ 9 8 4 2	♣ K Q J
73.	**73.**	**78.**	**78.**
S. opens 1♡.	S. opens 1♡.	N. opens 1♠.	N. opens 1♠.
♠ K Q 8	♠ 7 6 5	♠ A Q	♠ 7
♡ A Q	♡ 8 4 3	♡ A J 6	♡ K 9 2
◇ 7 6 4 2	◇ A Q	◇ K Q 9 4	◇ J 8 2
♣ A K 9 3	♣ Q 7 5 4 2	♣ 9 5 3 2	♣ K Q J 8 7 4

PLAY HANDS ON OVERCALLS AND DEFENSE

Hand 29 : Overcall — Leading partner's suit — Creating a void

Dealer North : Nil vulnerable

NORTH
♠ A K
♡ K 8 6 2
◇ K Q 10 9 3
♣ 10 5

WEST
♠ 10 9 8
♡ 4 3
◇ 8 7 6 5 2
♣ K 7 2

EAST
♠ 6 5 4 3
♡ 9 5
◇ A
♣ A Q J 8 6 3

SOUTH
♠ Q J 7 2
♡ A Q J 10 7
◇ J 4
♣ 9 4

WEST	NORTH	EAST	SOUTH
	1◇	2♣	2♡
Pass	4♡	All pass	

Bidding: East's suit is excellent and warrants the overcall. South's 2♡ shows 10 points or better, so that North, worth 17 in support of hearts, has no trouble raising to 4♡.

Lead: ♣2. Lead bottom from three or four to an honor.

Play: East should win ♣A, cash the ◇A to create a void and lead a low club. West wins the ♣K and East ruffs the diamond return. This plan would also work if West's ♣2 lead were a singleton, but if West wrongly led the king of clubs, 4♡ makes.

Hand 30 : Raising an overcall — Reading the lead — Creating a void

Dealer East : Nil vulnerable

NORTH
♠ 6 5
♡ 2
◇ J 7 6 4 3
♣ J 7 5 4 2

WEST
♠ K J 10 9 3
♡ K 9
◇ 10 5 2
♣ A Q 8

EAST
♠ Q 8 4 2
♡ Q J 10 7
◇ Q 9 8
♣ K 9

SOUTH
♠ A 7
♡ A 8 6 5 4 3
◇ A K
♣ 10 6 3

WEST	NORTH	EAST	SOUTH
		Pass	1♡
1♠	Pass	2♠	All pass

Bidding : As the top limit for an overcall is 15 HCP, East raises only to 2♠. Nobody should push higher.

Lead: ♡2. Partner's suit is normal.

Play : Winning ♡A, South notes that partner's lead is a singleton, as there is only one other heart missing and with a doubleton, partner would have led the top card, not the bottom. South cashes the A-K of diamonds (ace-then-king to show a doubleton), creating a void, and leads a heart for North to ruff. South ruffs the diamond return and the ♠A means one off.

Hand 31 : Raising an overcall – Third hand high – Finding a switch

Dealer South : Nil vulnerable

NORTH
♠ 5 2
♡ A 9 3 2
◇ 8 2
♣ J 9 8 6 4

WEST
♠ Q 10 3
♡ 8 5 4
◇ J 10 9 4
♣ K Q 7

EAST
♠ A K J 9 8 4
♡ K
◇ K 7 5
♣ 10 5 3

SOUTH
♠ 7 6
♡ Q J 10 7 6
◇ A Q 6 3
♣ A 2

WEST	NORTH	EAST	SOUTH
			1♡
Pass	2♡	2♠	3♡
3♠	Pass	Pass	Pass

Bidding : East has enough for 2♠ and South should compete to 3♡. Do not sell out at the 2-level with a trump fit. 3♡ would succeed but West raises partner to 3♠. 3-card support is enough to raise an overcall.

Lead : ♡Q. Top of sequence.

Play : Deducing that East holds ♡K, North plays the ace. When the ♡K drops, it is futile to continue hearts. North switches to ◇8, top from a doubleton. South wins and continues diamonds, North ruffing the third round, and ♣A defeats the contract.

Hand 32 : Reading the lead – Third hand high – Finding the switch

Dealer West : Nil vulnerable

NORTH
♠ A K
♡ A 10 9 8 5 2
◇ K 3
♣ K J 10

WEST
♠ 8 7 5 4 3 2
♡ 7 4
◇ A 7 5
♣ 9 4

EAST
♠ Q 6
♡ J
◇ Q J 10 9 6 4
♣ A Q 8 7

SOUTH
♠ J 10 9
♡ K Q 6 3
◇ 8 2
♣ 6 5 3 2

WEST	NORTH	EAST	SOUTH
Pass	1♡	2◇	2♡
Pass	4♡	All pass	

Bidding : East's good suit justifies the 2◇ overcall. West is too weak to raise to 3◇. After receiving support, North revalues to 20 points.

Lead : ◇Q. Top of sequence.

Play : From the lead, West knows declarer has the ◇K and plays the ◇A (third hand high). When the ◇K does not fall, West sees there are no more tricks coming in that suit for the defense. If returning partner's suit is clearly futile, it is generally better to switch. West switches to clubs, 9-then-4 with the doubleton, and ruffs the third club to defeat 4♡.

CHAPTER 11
TAKEOUT DOUBLES

If the opponents have opened the bidding and you have a strong hand, you will have a natural desire to get into the bidding. Yet if you lack a long suit to overcall and the hand is not suitable for a 1NT overcall, you should pass unless your hand meets *all* the requirements for a takeout double. Two basic types of doubles are commonly used : The Penalty Double *which asks partner to pass* (and aims to collect larger penalties by defeating the opponents' contract) and the Takeout Double *which asks partner to bid* (and aims to find a decent contract for your side). As the meaning of these two doubles is opposite, it is clearly vital to know when partner's double is for takeout and when it is for penalties.

In standard methods, a double is for penalties if :

(a) It is a double of a no-trump bid, *or*

(b) It is a double at the 3-level or higher.

Some partnerships change these conditions, but unless you and partner have some specific agreement to the contrary, a double under either of the above conditions is intended as a penalty double. Many partnerships play that a double of a pre-emptive opening at the 3-level is for takeout.

The general rule is that a double is for takeout if it is a double of a suit bid at the 1-level or the 2-level. A takeout double is usually made at first opportunity, but this need not be so. It is certainly possible to open the bidding and make a takeout double on the second round or to make an overcall initially and follow with a takeout double on the next round, provided that the above conditions for a takeout double are met.

WHAT YOU NEED TO MAKE A TAKEOUT DOUBLE :

A takeout double has point count requirements *and* shape requirements. The more strength you have, the more you may depart from the requirements of shape, but for a minimum strength double, the shape factors are vital.

When valuing your hand for a takeout double, count high card points and add 3-2-1 points for a shortage in the opposition's suit : 3 for a void, 2 for a singleton and 1 for a doubleton. If on this basis your hand measures 13 points or better, you have the minimum strength needed for a double.

The shape requirements for a takeout double are a shortage in the enemy suit (doubleton or shorter) plus support (four cards) in each unbid suit. It is permissible to have tolerance (three cards) in one of the unbid suits. Thus, if partner doubles one major, expect partner to have four cards in the other major, while if partner doubles a minor suit, expect at least 4-3 in the major suits. Holding both majors, double with 4-4, 5-4 or 5-5 in the majors, but prefer to overcall with 5-3 in the majors when the 5-card suit is strong.

Where the opponents have bid two suits, a takeout double shows support for both unbid suits. Where the doubler is a passed hand, the takeout double shows 9-11 HCP plus support for any unbid suit.

If the doubler has 16 HCP or more, the shape requirements are eased: the doubler need not have a shortage in the enemy suit and need have only tolerance in the unbid suits rather than support. Where the doubler has 19 HCP or more, there are no shape requirements for the double.

RESPONDING TO PARTNER'S TAKEOUT DOUBLE :

You are obliged to answer partner's takeout double no matter how weak a hand you have. The only time you might elect to pass a takeout double, and thus convert it to a penalty double, is when you have better trumps in your hand than the opponent who bid that suit. (Normally, you would need at least five trumps including three honors to pass out a takeout double.) For practical purposes, take partner's takeout double as forcing.

If you intend to bid a suit in answer to the double, count your HCP and add 5-3-1 shortage points (5 for a void, 3 for a singleton, 1 for a doubleton). If you intend to bid no-trumps, count only your high card points. After you have assessed the value of your hand, these are your options :

0-5   points : Bid a suit at the cheapest possible level.

6-9   points : Bid a suit at the cheapest possible level or bid 1NT.

10-12 points : Make a jump bid in a suit or bid 2NT.

13 points or more : Bid a game or bid the enemy suit to force to game.

A suit response thus has a range of 0-9 points. With the upper end of this range (6-9), try to bid a second time if a convenient opportunity arises. If the third player bids over partner's takeout double, and thus removes it, the obligation to reply to the double ceases. In such a case, you should pass with 0-5 points and make your normal reply with 6 points or more. When responding to a takeout double, ask yourself first "What shall I bid?" and after you have the answer to that, ask "How high shall I bid it?"

The order of priority when responding to a takeout double is :

● **Bid a major first.** Prefer a major suit to a longer or better minor.

● **With no major available, choose a no-trumps response if possible.** For a no-trumps response, you need at least one stopper in the enemy suit and some high card strength (6-9 points for 1NT). When you hold just 0-5 points, choose a suit bid. The 1NT response is not garbage.

● **If unable to bid a major or no-trumps, bid a minor.**

REBIDS BY THE DOUBLER :

(a) After a reply showing 0-9 points : The doubler revalues the hand if a trump fit is located, adding the 5-3-1 shortage count to the high card points. Then with 13-16 points, the doubler should pass. With 17-19 points, the doubler should bid again, and with 20-22 points, the doubler should make a jump-rebid. When the doubler bids again, partner should keep bidding with the 6-9 point hand and pass with 0-5, while if the doubler has made a jump-rebid, partner should bid to a game if holding one sure winner.

(b) After a response showing 10-12 points : Pass with just 12-13 points, but bid on with 14 points or more and head for a game with 16 or more.

(c) A second bid by the doubler is always a strong action, showing at least 16 points. A change of suit by the doubler shows a 5-card or longer suit and denies support for the suit bid by partner. A no-trump rebid by the doubler shows 19-21 points and a balanced hand (since with 16-18 balanced, you would make an immediate overcall of 1NT, while with 13-15 you would not want to bid again after doubling if partner has shown a hand of 0-9 points). A new suit by the doubler is not forcing if partner has shown 0-9 points, but is forcing if partner made a reply showing 10-12 points.

ACTION BY THIRD HAND AFTER A TAKEOUT DOUBLE :

The standard approach after partner has opened and second player makes a takeout double is for third player to pass on a weak hand, bid in the normal way with 6 points or better and redouble with 10 HCP or more. After the redouble, the partner of the doubler should make the normal reply (as the redouble has not removed the double) and the opener should usually pass, unless the hand is suitable to double the last bid for penalties. The redouble promises another bid, so that the opener can pass in safety, even with a good hand, knowing that the redoubler will bid again. After a redouble, any double by the opener or the redoubler is a penalty double. The function of the redouble is to confirm that your side has more points than they do and thus you can capitalise on the jeopardy in which the opponents find themselves.

EXERCISES ON TAKEOUT DOUBLES

A. In the following auctions, is West's double for takeout or for penalties?

1.				2.				3.			
N	E	S	W	N	E	S	W	N	E	S	W
No	No	1♡	Dbl	1♢	No	1♠	Dbl	1♡	No	2♡	Dbl

4.				5.				6.			
N	E	S	W	N	E	S	W	N	E	S	W
No	1♡	4♠	Dbl		No	1NT	Dbl			1NT 2♠	Dbl

B. You are East. North opens 1♣. What action do you take on these hands?

1.	♠ K 8 4 3	2.	♠ A J 8 7	3.	♠ A Q 8 7
	♡ Q J 4 2		♡ Q 9 4 3		♡ 6
	♢ A Q 7 2		♢ A 10 7 4 3		♢ A K 10 4 3 2
	♣ 5		♣ - - -		♣ 6 2

4.	♠ A K J 4	5.	♠ A Q J 9 6 5	6.	♠ A Q 8 7 5
	♡ A J 9 6 3		♡ K Q J		♡ 6
	♢ K 2		♢ A K		♢ A K 10 4 3
	♣ 7 4		♣ 5 2		♣ 4 3

7.	♠ A J 9 7	8.	♠ A J 6 2	9.	♠ A 7
	♡ K Q 9		♡ K Q 7		♡ K J 2
	♢ A 8 4 3		♢ J 9 6		♢ A Q J 5
	♣ 6 3		♣ A Q 5		♣ K Q 3 2

C. You are East. North opens 1♡. What action do you take on these hands?

1.	♠ K J 7	2.	♠ K Q	3.	♠ K Q 7 2
	♡ A 8		♡ A 4 3		♡ A 3
	♢ Q 4 3 2		♢ A 8 3 2		♢ A 8 3 2
	♣ Q 9 6 3		♣ J 7 5 4		♣ J 7 5

4.	♠ A K 10 9 6	5.	♠ J 8 3 2	6.	♠ K
	♡ 3		♡ 6		♡ A K 10 9 6 2
	♢ A 5 4		♢ A K 7 6 2		♢ A 7 4
	♣ Q 8 6 3		♣ K Q 9		♣ J 4 3

7.	♠ A Q	8.	♠ A Q	9.	♠ A Q J 6 2
	♡ K 9 3		♡ K 9 3		♡ A 4
	♢ A J 4 3		♢ A K 4 3		♢ A K J 5
	♣ K 8 7 4		♣ K J 7 4		♣ Q 3

D. **N**   **E**   **S**   **W**   The bidding has started as on the left.
    1♦   Dbl   No   ?   What action should West take on these hands?

1. ♠ K 9 7 3
   ♡ Q 5
   ♦ 7 6 4 3
   ♣ 8 3 2

2. ♠ 9 7 3 2
   ♡ 8 4 2
   ♦ 7 6
   ♣ 9 6 4 2

3. ♠ Q 9 8 7 4
   ♡ Q 8 6 5
   ♦ 4 3
   ♣ 6 2

4. ♠ 6 2
   ♡ Q 8 6 5
   ♦ 4 3
   ♣ Q 9 8 7 4

5. ♠ A 7 6
   ♡ 9 2
   ♦ 4 3 2
   ♣ J 9 8 6 3

6. ♠ 7 6 4
   ♡ 5 4 3
   ♦ 7 6 4 3 2
   ♣ 3 2

E. **N**   **E**   **S**   **W**   The bidding has started as on the left.
    1♣   Dbl   No   ?   What action should West take on these hands?

1. ♠ K 9 8 4 3
   ♡ 6
   ♦ 6 4 2
   ♣ A 7 4 2

2. ♠ K 9 5 4
   ♡ A J 10 7 5
   ♦ 4 3
   ♣ 6 2

3. ♠ 7 6
   ♡ K 8 4
   ♦ A Q J 4 2
   ♣ 6 5 3

4. ♠ J 8 4
   ♡ A 7 3
   ♦ 8 5 3 2
   ♣ Q J 5

5. ♠ 8 5
   ♡ A 7 2
   ♦ A J 9 3
   ♣ Q 10 8 7

6. ♠ K Q 8 7 4 3
   ♡ A 8
   ♦ 2
   ♣ 7 6 4 3

F. **N**   **E**   **S**   **W**   The bidding has started as on the left.
    1♦   Dbl   1♠   ?   What action should West take on these hands?

1. ♠ Q 7
   ♡ Q 8 4 3
   ♦ 9 6 2
   ♣ 8 6 5 2

2. ♠ 7 2
   ♡ Q J 8 4
   ♦ 8 6 5
   ♣ K J 8 7

3. ♠ 9
   ♡ A J 9 8 5
   ♦ 7 6 2
   ♣ K 8 7 2

G. **N**   **E**   **S**   **W**   The bidding has started as on the left.
    No   No   1♦   Dbl   What action should West take on these hands?
    No   1♡   No   ?

1. ♠ A J 7 4
   ♡ K Q 4 2
   ♦ 7 6
   ♣ K 8 2

2. ♠ A J 7 3
   ♡ K Q 4 2
   ♦ 7 6
   ♣ A K 3

3. ♠ A 8 2
   ♡ A K Q 3
   ♦ K Q 9 8 2
   ♣ 6

PARTNERSHIP BIDDING PRACTICE
FEATURING TAKEOUT DOUBLES

There is no North-South bidding other than that shown.

WEST	EAST	WEST	EAST
79.	**79.**	**84.**	**84.**
N. opens 1♡.	N. opens 1♡.	N. opens 1♡.	N. opens 1♡.
♠ J 7	♠ K Q 4 3	♠ K J 7	♠ A Q 9 3
♡ 8 6 4 2	♡ 7	♡ A J 10	♡ 7 2
◇ Q 7 5 3	◇ A J 8 6	◇ 7 6 3	◇ A 9 2
♣ 10 6 5	♣ Q 9 8 3	♣ 8 7 4 2	♣ A Q J 5
80.	**80.**	**85.**	**85.**
S. opens 1♡.	S. opens 1♡.	S. opens 1♠.	S. opens 1♠.
♠ A K 7 6	♠ 10 8 4	♠ 7	♠ A 8 5 2
♡ 8 3	♡ 9 7 6	♡ A Q 8 3	♡ J 10 2
◇ A Q 9	◇ 4 3	◇ K Q 9 3	◇ A 7 4
♣ J 7 6 4	♣ K 9 5 3 2	♣ A J 9 2	♣ Q 8 3
81.	**81.**	**86.**	**86.**
S. opens 1♣.	S. opens 1♣.	S. opens 1♡.	S. opens 1♡.
♠ A K J 6	♠ Q 9 4 3	♠ A 8 6 2	♠ K Q 9 7 5
♡ K Q J 4	♡ 8 7	♡ 7 4	♡ A 2
◇ A 4 3	◇ 9 8 5 2	◇ A K 6 2	◇ 7 4 3
♣ 9 2	♣ 8 7 6	♣ J 8 5	♣ 9 6 3
82.	**82.**	**87.**	**87.**
N. opens 1♣.	N. opens 1♣.	N. opens 1♣.	N. opens 1♣.
♠ 9 7	♠ A K 5 2	♠ K Q J 6 5 2	♠ A 7 4 3
♡ 6 5 4 2	♡ K Q J 7 3	♡ 7 5	♡ A 9 8 2
◇ 7 6 4	◇ K Q	◇ K J	◇ A 5 4 3
♣ J 8 3 2	♣ 9 7	♣ Q 6 2	♣ 7
83.	**83.**	**88.**	**88.**
N. opens 1◇.	N. opens 1◇.	S. opens 1◇.	S. opens 1◇.
♠ K Q 8 7	♠ A 9 6 3	♠ A K J 7	♠ 6 4
♡ 7 6	♡ K Q 8 5	♡ A 10 9 6 2	♡ K 8 3
◇ 5 4	◇ 9 6	◇ 9	◇ J 6 5
♣ 8 6 4 3 2	♣ A 7 5	♣ A 6 2	♣ K Q J 8 3

PLAY HANDS ON TAKEOUT DOUBLES

Hand 33 : Leading towards honor cards when two honors are missing

Dealer North : Nil vulnerable

	NORTH	EAST	SOUTH
	Pass	Pass	1♣
Dble	Pass	2♡	Pass
4♡	Pass	Pass	Pass

WEST NORTH EAST SOUTH

```
            NORTH
            ♠ J 10 8 7 4 3
            ♡ 6
            ◇ 10 9 5
            ♣ J 5 3
WEST                     EAST
♠ K Q 6 5                ♠ A 2
♡ K Q 5 4                ♡ 9 8 7 3 2
◇ A J 6 4                ◇ K 3
♣ 4                      ♣ Q 10 6 2
            SOUTH
            ♠ 9
            ♡ A J 10
            ◇ Q 8 7 2
            ♣ A K 9 8 7
```

Bidding : East's 2♡ jump reply to the double shows 10-12 points.

Lead : ♣K, normal from A-K suits.

Play : South switches to the ♠9. East wins and leads a heart to the K, winning. As South is marked with the ♡A, do not lead a second heart from dummy. A diamond to the K and another heart is led *towards* dummy. This holds the defense to just one trump trick. One club loser can be ruffed later and another discarded on the third spade.

Hand 34 : Delaying trumps to take a quick discard

Dealer East : E-W vulnerable

WEST	NORTH	EAST	SOUTH
		1◇	Dble
Pass	4♡	All pass	

```
            NORTH
            ♠ 8
            ♡ K J 10 6 5 4
            ◇ A 6
            ♣ J 9 6 2
WEST                     EAST
♠ Q 9 7 2                ♠ J 5 4 3
♡ 7                      ♡ A Q 2
◇ 10 9 7 3               ◇ K Q J 8 4
♣ 10 8 5 3               ♣ Q
            SOUTH
            ♠ A K 10 6
            ♡ 9 8 3
            ◇ 5 2
            ♣ A K 7 4
```

Bidding: North is worth 13 points, (3 for the singleton and 1 for the doubleton). With 13 points or more opposite a double, you should reach a game and 4♡ is the clear choice.

Lead : ◇ K. Prefer the sequence.

Play : Win ◇ A, play the ♠A and ♠K to discard the diamond loser. Then lead a trump, finessing the jack. Declarer should keep on with trumps until all are drawn. West should keep the clubs ('keep length with dummy'). When East shows out on the second club, North finesses ♣9 if necessary.

Hand 35 : Signalling with a doubleton — Card reading by declarer

Dealer South : Both vulnerable

WEST	NORTH	EAST	SOUTH
			Pass
1◇	Dble	Pass	1♡
Pass	2♡	All pass	

NORTH
♠ A K Q J
♡ K 7 5 3
◇ K
♣ Q 4 3 2

WEST
♠ 8 5
♡ Q 9
◇ Q J 7 5 2
♣ A K J 8

EAST
♠ 10 9 7 4 2
♡ 10 8 6
◇ A 10 3
♣ 9 5

SOUTH
♠ 6 3
♡ A J 4 2
◇ 9 8 6 4
♣ 10 7 6

Bidding: Opposite 0-9 points, North is worth a mild try for game and raises to 2♡, but South is too weak to bid on.

Lead: ♣K. A-K leads are attractive.

Play: East signals with the ♣9 to continue clubs and ruffs the third round of clubs. East cashes the ◇ A and exits with a diamond or a spade. With only 17 HCP missing and the ◇ A with East, the ♡ Q is marked with West. South refuses the normal finesse for the queen when holding 8 trumps and plays ♡K and ♡A. The ♡ Q luckily drops — 9 tricks.

Hand 36 : Card reading — Finessing — Careful use of entries

Dealer West : Both vulnerable

WEST	NORTH	EAST	SOUTH
Pass	1♠	Dble	Pass
2NT	Pass	3NT	All pass

NORTH
♠ K Q J 10 7
♡ K 8 6 2
◇ 9 4
♣ A 10

WEST
♠ A 9 3 2
♡ 7 4 3
◇ K J 8
♣ Q J 5

EAST
♠ 5
♡ A Q J 10
◇ A Q 5 2
♣ K 8 7 2

SOUTH
♠ 8 6 4
♡ 9 5
◇ 10 7 6 3
♣ 9 6 4 3

Bidding : West's 2NT denies four hearts and shows 10-12 points, balanced, with at least one stopper in spades. East has enough to try for game and 3NT looks the best bet.

Lead : ♠K. To set up the spades.

Play : After winning ♠A, West should realise that it is futile to go for the clubs. North will win and cash the rest of the spades. As only 13 HCP are missing, North is marked with the ♡K for the opening bid. So, finesse the ♡ Q, diamond to the jack, finesse the ♡ J, diamond to the king, finesse the ♡10 and you have 9 tricks.

CHAPTER 12
PENALTY DOUBLES

When you are confident that you can defeat the opponents' contract, it is highly attractive to double them because the bonus points you receive by way of penalties mount up quickly if you can beat them by more than one trick. If they are not vulnerable, you collect 50 points for every trick by which they fail, but if you have doubled them, you collect 100 for one down and 200 for each additional trick. If they are vulnerable, it is even more lucrative to double them. Undoubled, they lose only 100 per trick for failure, but if doubled, the penalties are 200 for one down and 300 for each additional trick. Three down doubled not vulnerable or two down doubled vulnerable amounts to 500, the same score as completing the rubber by two games to one.

On the other hand, if they make their contract doubled, they score double points, plus 50 for the insult of being doubled. In addition, overtricks made when doubled are more valuable than usual: 100 points per overtrick when not vulnerable and 200 points per overtrick when vulnerable. Consider also that if they redouble and make it, the preceding scores are doubled again. Thus, when you do double you need to be fairly sure that you can defeat them.

When To Double Their 1NT Opening

You should hold at least as many points as they do. If they are using the strong 1NT, double if you hold 17 HCP or more. If they are using the weak 1NT (12-14 HCP or 13-15 HCP), double if holding 15 HCP or more. Partner is expected to pass your double, but with a dreadful hand and a long suit, partner is permitted to remove your double and bid the long suit. This removal of the penalty double is done only on a very weak hand. If either opponent bids a suit after their 1NT has been doubled, you or partner should double this with a strong 4-card or better holding in that suit.

When To Double Their 1NT Overcall

When partner has opened and second player overcalls 1NT, double if your side has more points than they do. If they are trying for more than half the tricks with less than half the points, they will usually fail. Therefore, to maximise your score, double their 1NT overcall whenever you hold 9 HCP or better. Again, after their 1NT has been doubled, if either opponent tries to escape by bidding a suit, you or partner should double this rescue attempt with a strong 4-card holding in the suit they have bid.

When To Double Their Suit Overcall At The One-Level

To extract a decent penalty at the 1-level, you need excellent trumps. To defeat them at all, you will have to take seven tricks. This is equivalent to making a contract of one or more in their suit with a known bad break. Consequently, your trumps should be better than theirs and the minimum recommended is five trumps with three honors. It is also helpful to have a shortage in the suit partner opened and at least 20 HCP for your side.

When To Double Their Suit Overcall At The Two-Level

The requirements are slightly less but you still should be strong in their trump suit. For a double at the 2-level, you should hold :
● At least 20 HCP between you and partner, *and*
● Four or more trumps, including at least two honors, *and*
● A shortage in partner's suit, preferably a singleton.

When To Double Their Suit At The Three-Level

As doubles above $2\diamondsuit$ give them a game if they succeed, you need to be very confident you will defeat them. For a penalty double at the three-level, you should have six or more tricks between you and partner, including at least one trump trick. Partner should hold 1-2 tricks with 6-10 HCP and 2-3 tricks with 11-15 HCP. Add your own winners to this expectancy.

If you are highly likely to make a game, do not settle for a small penalty. Rather bid on to your best game. If you can make a game, you need at least 500 points from the double as compensation for the game missed.

When To Double Their Game Contracts

If they bid above your game, double if your side has more points. However, if they have bid to a game without interference, you normally do not double, even though you hope to defeat them. Points are not enough. If they have a singleton or a void, your expected winners might vanish. The best time to double their game is if they have barely enough for game (they had an invitational auction like $1\heartsuit : 1NT, 2\diamondsuit : 2\heartsuit, 3\heartsuit : 4\heartsuit$) *and* you know they are in for a bad break in trumps. Double and collect big.

When To Double Their Slams

Almost never double, even if you know you can defeat them! You might collect an extra 50 or 100 *if* you beat them, but they might collect an extra 230 (or 590 if they redouble) if they make it. Even with Q-J-10-9 in trumps, just pass and be satisfied to defeat them. If you double, they might bid some other slam, such as 6NT, which you are unable to beat. What a disaster!

APPENDIX 1 : FROM WHIST TO BRIDGE

The following is suitable as an introduction to those who have never played bridge before. It includes a series of games leading almost to bridge.

WHAT TYPE OF GAME IS BRIDGE?

There are two basic families of card games. In one, the aim is to form combinations of cards, e.g. Gin Rummy, Canasta. Contract Bridge belongs to the other in which the aim is to win *tricks*. Other games in the bridge family are Solo, Five Hundred, Whist and Euchre.

Bridge is played by four people, two playing as partners, against the other two. Partners sit opposite each other. You will need a card table, four chairs, preferably two packs of cards (though you can manage with one pack), score pads and pencils.

HOW MANY CARDS ARE IN THE PACK?

A pack (or deck) of 52 cards is used. There is no joker. There are four suits: spades ♠, hearts ♡, diamonds ◇ and clubs ♣. Each suit has thirteen cards, the highest being the ace, followed by the king, queen, jack, 10, 9, 8, 7, 6, 5, 4, 3, down to the 2 which is the lowest.

HOW DO WE CHOOSE PARTNERS?

You may agree to play in certain partnerships, but it is usual to draw for partners. This is done by spreading out one pack, face down, and each player picking a card. The two who draw the higher cards play as partners against the other two, normally for one or two 'rubbers'. Then, cards are drawn again to form two new partnerships. If, in drawing for partners, two or more cards of the same rank are turned up, then the tie is split according to suit, the suits ranking from the highest, spades, through hearts and diamonds to the lowest, clubs.

WHO DEALS?

The player who drew the highest card has the right to choose seats (the most comfortable one) and which pack of cards to use for dealing (for the supersititiously inclined, who might think that one pack is the luckier), and also becomes the dealer on the first hand. The next dealer will be the player on the left of the previous dealer and so on in clockwise rotation.

The cards are shuffled by the player on the dealer's left who passes them across the table to the player on the dealer's right to 'cut' them. The dealer completes the 'cut' and then 'deals' the cards, one at a time, face down, in clockwise direction, starting with the player on the left, until all 52 are dealt.

It is customary etiquette not to pick up your cards until the dealer has finished dealing... this allows the dealer the same time to study the cards as everyone else has and also allows a misdeal to be corrected. During the deal, the dealer's partner is shuffling the other pack in preparation for the next deal... that is why two packs are used, in order to speed up the game. After the shuffling is finished, the cards are placed on the the shuffler's right, ready for the next dealer to pick up.

THE START OF PLAY

After picking up your 13 cards, sort them into suits... it is usual to separate the red suits from the black suits and also to put your cards in order of rank in each suit. The bidding starts with the dealer but more about the bidding later.

GAME 1 – WHIST

Each player receives 13 cards. Opposite players are partners. There is no bidding yet. The top card of the other pack is turned face up. If it is a 2, 3 or 4, the hand is to be played at no-trumps. If it is a 5 or higher, the suit of the face-up card will be trumps for that deal. The player on the left of the dealer makes the first lead, that is, places one card face up on the table. Each player plays a card face up in turn in clockwise order. That group of four cards, one from each player, is called a *trick*. *Each player must follow suit if possible.* If you are unable to follow suit, at no-trumps you should discard those cards which you judge to be worthless, but when there is a trump suit, you are permitted to play a trump card which beats any card in any other suit.

A trick with no trump card is won by the highest card in the suit led. A trick with a trump card is won by the highest trump card on the trick. You may play a high card or a low card but if possible, you must follow suit. One situation where you could win the trick but it could be foolish to do so is if partner's card has already won the trick.

Play continues until all 13 tricks have been played and each side then counts up the number of tricks won. The side winning more than 6 tricks is the winner and is the only side that scores points.

SCORING :

The first partnership to score **100 points or more** in tricks won scores a **GAME.** We play a **RUBBER** of bridge and a rubber is **best of three games.** The first partnership to win two games wins the rubber. A 2-0 win scores 700 bonus points, a 2-1 wins scores 500 bonus points.

SCORING AT NO-TRUMPS :

30 points for each trick won over six, plus 10.

SCORING AT TRUMPS :

With Spades or Hearts as trumps : 30 points for each trick over six.
With Diamonds or Clubs as trumps : 20 points for each trick over six.

A bridge scoresheet looks like this :

```
WE  |  THEY
    |
    |
    |
B O N|U S E S
T R I|C K S
    |
    |
    |
    |
    |
    |
```

Trick scores are written below the line, bonus scores are written above the line. At the end of a game, a line is ruled across both columns and both sides start the next game from zero again. At the end of a rubber the scores in each column are tallied and the side scoring more points is the winner. The difference between the two scores is rounded off to the nearest 100 (e.g. 870 goes to 900, 820 goes to 800; 850 would go down to 800) and the score is then entered as the number of 100s won or lost. For example, if you won by 930, your scoresheet reads '+9' while their scoresheet would record '−9'.

GUIDELINES FOR PLAY AT NO-TRUMPS :

Prefer to lead your longest suit and keep on with that suit. When the others run out, your remaining cards in that suit will be winners, since they cannot win the trick if they cannot follow suit. As players lead their own long suit, prefer to return partner's led suit, unless you have a strong suit of your own, and usually avoid returning a suit led by the opposition.

Second player to a trick commonly plays low, third player normally plays high. If partner's card has already won the trick, you need not play high.

The card to lead : Top card from a sequence of three or more cards headed by the ten or higher (e.g. from K-Q-J-5, lead the K; from J-10-9-8, lead the J).

Lead fourth-highest (fourth from the top) when the long suit has no three-card or longer sequence. (e.g. from K-J-8-4-3, lead the 4).

GUIDELINES FOR PLAY AT TRUMPS :

Leading the longest suit is no longer so attractive. Prefer to lead a strong suit (headed by a *sequence* or by A-K) or a singleton (so you can trump in). With plenty of trumps, lead trumps to remove the opponents trump cards so that they cannot trump your winners. If you lead a doubleton (two cards in the suit), standard technique is to lead top card from a doubleton.

After a few of these games, move on to Game 2.

GAME 2 – DUMMY WHIST

Each player receives 13 cards and counts the high card points (HCP), using **A = 4, K = 3, Q = 2** and **J = 1.** Starting with the dealer, each player calls out the total number of points held. The side which has more points becomes the declarer side and the partner that has more points becomes the declarer. (The pack has 40 HCP. If each side has 20, redeal the hand. For a tie within the declarer side, the player nearer the dealer will be the declarer.)

The declarer's partner is known as the 'dummy' and the dummy hand is placed face up on the table, neatly in suits facing declarer. Declarer will nominate the trump suit or no-trumps. To choose a trump suit, the suit should have 8 or more cards in the combined hands. If more than one trump suit is available, choose a major suit (spades or hearts) rather than a minor suit (diamonds or clubs), as the majors score more. If the suits are both majors or both minors, choose the longer, or if both have the same length, choose the stronger. With no suit which has 8 or more trumps together, play no-trumps.

After the trump suit or no-trumps has been declared, the player on the left of the declarer makes the first lead. The play proceeds as before but **the declarer must play both hands.** The dummy player takes no part in the play. If dummy wins a trick, the next lead comes from dummy, while if declarer wins a trick, declarer must lead to the next trick.

SCORING :

If declarer scores seven tricks or more, scoring is as usual. If declarer fails to win seven tricks, the opponents score bonus points. *Only the declarer side can score points for game.* Where the declarer side has not won a game ('not vulnerable'), the opponents score 50 points for each trick by which they have defeated declarer, regardless of which suit is trumps or whether no-trumps is played. Where the declarer side has won one game ('vulnerable'), the opponents score 100 points for each trick by which they have defeated declarer.

Bonus points, scored above the line, do not count towards a game. They are still valuable since they count in your total points at the end of the rubber.

The existence of the dummy marks off Bridge from other trick-taking games. From the first lead, each player sees half the pack (13 cards in hand and the 13 cards in dummy), thus making Bridge essentially a game of skill, in contrast to the large luck factor in the other games. Since the declarer side in this game will have more points than the defenders, the declarer side is more likely to succeed in taking seven or more tricks.

After a few of these games, move on to Game 3.

GAME 3 — BIDDING WHIST

Starting with the dealer, each player states the number of points held. The side with more points is the declarer side and the two partners discuss which suit shall be trumps or whether to play no-trumps. Each partner in turn suggests a trump suit or no-trumps, until agreement is reached. This is known as the 'bidding' or the 'auction'. A bid is simply a suggestion to partner which suit you prefer as trumps or whether you prefer no-trumps.

A suggested trump suit must contain at least four cards. With no long suit and with no void or singleton, it is usually best to suggest no-trumps at once. If there is no early agreement and neither partner insists on a suit, one of the partners should suggest no-trumps. After agreement, the first player to suggest the agreed trump suit (or no-trumps if agreed) is the declarer.

The player on the left of the declarer makes the opening lead *before seeing dummy*. After the lead, dummy's 13 cards are placed face up (in suits), facing declarer. Trumps go on dummy's right. The scoring is the same as for Game 2.

GAME 4 — CONTRACT WHIST

Proceed as for Game 3 above, but the declarer is required to win a specific number of tricks depending on the total points held by declarer and dummy:

20-22 points :	7 or more tricks in no-trumps
	8 or more tricks with a trump suit
23-25 points :	8 or more tricks in no-trumps
	9 or more tricks with a trump suit
26-32 points :	9 or more tricks in no-trumps
	10 or more tricks with ♡ or ♠ as trumps
	11 or more tricks with ♣ or ♢ as trumps
33-36 points :	12 or more tricks
37-40 points :	All 13 tricks

PLAY : The opening lead is made before dummy appears.

SCORING : As for Game 2, but declarer must win the number of tricks stipulated or more. If not, the defenders score 50 (declarer not vulnerable) or 100 (declarer vulnerable) for each trick by which declarer fails.

If required to win 12 tricks the declarer side if successful scores an extra 500 not vulnerable or 750 vulnerable. If required to win all 13 tricks, the declarer side if successful scores an extra 1000 not vulnerable or 1500 vulnerable.

If extra time is available, more games similar to these can be played.

APPENDIX 2 : THE STAYMAN CONVENTION

All players of experience know and understand the Stayman Convention, a response of 2♣ to a 1NT opening. The Stayman 2♣ is designed to locate the best game contract in a major suit with a 4-4 fit in preference to no-trumps. After you have been playing for some time, you will want to include Stayman in your system, since Stayman is part and parcel of all standard systems.

The 2♣ response to 1NT asks partner, "Do you have a 4-card major?" If opener has a major, opener bids it (bidding 2♡ if opener has two 4-card majors), while the negative reply, denying a 4-card major, is 2◊.

WHEN TO USE STAYMAN :

Use the 2♣ reply to 1NT when you hold :

● Enough points to invite a game, and

● One 4-card major *or* both majors, 4-4, 5-4 or 5-5

REPLIES TO 2♣ STAYMAN :

2◊ = No major suit

2♡ = 4 hearts (may have spades also)

2♠ = 4 spades (will not have four hearts)

AFTER OPENER'S REPLY TO STAYMAN :

A new suit by responder is a 5-card suit and a jump-bid is forcing to game (e.g. 1NT : 2♣, 2◊ : 3♠ would show five spades and enough for game). If opener has bid one major, a bid of no-trumps by responder would show that responder had four cards in the other major. Responder's rebid of 2NT invites game (like 1NT : 2NT immediately), and raising opener's major suit to the 3-level likewise invites game and shows support of opener's major.

STAYMAN WITH WEAK RESPONDING HANDS :

When responder bids 2♣ over 1NT and rebids 3♣ over opener's answer, responder is showing 6 or more clubs and a very weak hand (not enough for a game). Opener is expected to pass. Responder's rebid of 2-in-a-major is also a weak rebid, showing a 5-card suit. Opener would normally pass but may raise the major with 3-card support and a maximum 1NT opening.

STAYMAN OVER A 2NT OPENING :

The 3♣ response to a 2NT opening operates in the same way as Stayman over 1NT, except that opener's replies occur at the 3-level. To use Stayman over 2NT, responder should have enough strength for game and either one 4-card major or both majors. A new suit rebid by responder after the reply to Stayman would be at least a 5-card suit and would be forcing.

APPENDIX 3 : OPENING LEADS — THE SUIT TO LEAD

(1) AGAINST NO-TRUMP CONTRACTS :

Under normal circumstances, the best strategy is to lead your longest suit and both defenders continue with that suit at every opportunity unless from the preceding play it has become clearly futile to pursue that suit.

Lead your own longest suit, *but*
Prefer to lead a long suit bid by partner, *and*
Avoid leading a suit which has been genuinely bid by the opponents.

Where partner has not bid a suit and your long suit has been bid by the opponents, choose another long suit if you have one, but if not, be prepared to lead even a 3-card suit. When faced with this decision to lead a short suit, prefer a major to a minor, longer to shorter and stronger to weaker.

(2) AGAINST TRUMP CONTRACTS :

It is no longer attractive to lead your long suit, since declarer or dummy is likely to ruff this suit after one or two rounds. Prefer one of these highly attractive leads :

A suit headed by a solid sequence, such as K-Q-J, Q-J-10, J-10-9, etc.
A suit headed by A-K-Q or A-K, *or*
A singleton, *or*
A suit bid by partner.

If none of these attractive leads exists, avoid these dreadful leads :

A suit headed by the ace without the king as well, *or*
Doubleton honors, such as K-x, Q-x, J-x, *or*
A singleton trump, *or*
A suit bid by the opposition.

If you still have more than one suit left after eliminating the terrible leads :

Lead a suit with two honors rather than a suit with just one honor.
Lead a doubleton rather than a suit with just one honor.
Lead a suit with no honors rather than a suit with just one honor.

A trump lead is reasonable from two or three worthless trumps if there is no evidence from the bidding that dummy holds a long suit.

If dummy is known to hold a long suit, lead an unbid suit. If you have just one honor card in the possible suits to lead, prefer a suit with the king to a suit with the queen; prefer a suit with the queen to a suit with the jack; prefer a suit with the jack to a suit with just the ace.

If you hold four or more trumps, lead your longest suit outside trumps to try to force declarer to ruff and reduce declarer's trump length.

APPENDIX 4 : OPENING LEADS — THE CARD TO LEAD

The basic rules are : top from a doubleton; from three cards, bottom with an honor, middle with no honor, top of two or three touching cards headed by an honor; from four or more cards, fourth-highest but lead top from solid sequences or near sequences and top of the touching honors when holding three honors. In the list that follows, the card to lead is the same whether you are leading partner's suit or your own suit. The lead is the same for a trump contract or for no-trumps except for those marked with an asterisk.

Holding	Lead	Holding	Lead	Holding	Lead
9 5	9	Q J 10 2	Q	A K	A
9 5 3	5	Q J 9 2	Q	A 6	A
9 6 5 3 2	3	Q J 8 2	2	A K Q	K
10 9	10	Q 10 9 8	10	A K J	K
10 6	10	Q 10 8 3	3	A K 3	K
10 9 3	10	Q 9 8 7 6	7	A 9 3**	A
10 6 3	3	Q 8 6 5 2	5	A K Q 3	K
10 6 3 2	2	K Q	K	A K J 3	K
10 9 8 3	10	K 2	K	A K 6 3*	K
10 9 7 3	10	K Q 5	K	A Q J 3***	A
10 9 6 3	3	K J 10	J	A Q 6 3*	A
J 10	J	K J 5	5	A J 10 3***	A
J 5	J	K 10 9	10	A J 6 3*	A
J 10 6	J	K 10 5	5	A 10 9 8***	A
J 5 2	2	K 7 5	5	A 10 5 2*	A
J 5 4 2	2	K Q J 2	K	A 9 8 7*	A
J 9 8 7 6	7	K Q 10 2	K	A 9 6 3*	A
J 7 5 4 2	4	K Q 9 2*	K	A K J 4 2	K
J 10 9 4	J	K J 10 2	J	A K 7 4 2*	K
J 10 8 4	J	K J 9 2	2	A Q J 4 2***	A
J 10 7 4	4	K 10 9 8	10	A Q 10 9 2***	A
Q J	Q	K 10 8 4	4	A Q 10 4 2*	A
Q 4	Q	K Q J 6 3	K	A Q 6 4 2*	A
Q J 4	Q	K Q 10 6 3	K	A J 10 5 3***	A
Q 10 9	10	K Q 7 6 3*	K	A J 8 5 3*	A
Q 10 4	4	K 9 8 7 3	7	A 10 9 8 3***	A
Q 6 4	4	K 8 6 4 3	4	A 10 8 5 3*	A

*Lead fourth-highest against no-trumps.
**Lead bottom against no-trumps.
***Lead the top of the touching honors against no-trumps, e.g. Q from AQJxx, J from AJ10xx, 10 from A109, A1098 or AQ109x, and so on.

APPENDIX 5 : NEGATIVE DOUBLES

Introduction : In former standard methods if partner had made a bid, a subsequent double by you was for penalties. Thus if the bidding had started with 1 ◇ from partner, an overcall of 1♠ by right-hand opponent and you doubled, it would mean that you had very strong spades (and 5 or 6 of them) and felt that 1♠ doubled was the best spot for your side.

The negative double is a variation of this approach. The definition of the negative double : double by responder after partner has opened with a suit bid and second player has intervened with a suit bid is for takeout, not for penalties. The method was devised by Alvin Roth in the late 1950s and today has become one of the cornerstones of successful competitive bidding.

Without the negative double many hands become difficult and even impossible to bid sensibly after opposition interference. This is particularly so because of the very strict requirements for a 2-level response (10 points or more). Suppose you picked up ♠ A765   ♡ K642   ◇ 763   ♣ 87 and partner opened 1 ◇. You intend to respond 1♡, allowing the partnership to find any available major suit fit. However, when second player intervenes with 2♣, you are too weak to respond at the 2-level and in standard methods you would have to pass. Obviously a good fit in either major could be lost.

Similarly, if you held   ♠ 76   ♡ K874   ◇ A732   ♣ 852 and the bidding commenced 1♣ from partner, 1♠ on your right, you would be lost and the hearts might likewise be lost in standard methods, since there is no satisfactory response (too weak for 2♡ or 2◇, support too poor for 2♣ and the absence of a stopper in spades makes 1NT unattractive).

The solution : Using a double by responder as a takeout bid solves many of these problems. It certainly makes competitive bidding far simpler and far more efficient. On the first hand above, responder would double 2♣ for takeout, showing both majors (as a takeout double normally does). If partner did have a fit in either major it would be known at once and partner could bid as high as the cards warranted. Likewise on the second hand, responder would double 1♠, showing 4 or more hearts (as a takeout double of 1♠ usually does) and if partner also had 4 hearts, the fit would be discovered at once.

Partnership agreements : In order to use negative doubles, you should agree with your partner *in advance* that you will use them. Initially you should adopt them only after an intervening suit bid at the 1-level or 2-level. You should also agree that a negative double shows 6 points or more, the normal requirements for a response at the 1-level. Opener will assume that the range for the negative double is 6-9 points (minimum response) and if responder in fact holds a stronger hand, responder will have to continue with a strong action later. Over interference, a change of suit is forcing, just as it normally is. Above the level of 2♠, doubles are for penalties.

Specific situations :

(a) Minor-Minor : Partner opens with a minor suit and they overcall in a minor suit, for example 1♣ : (1◇), or 1◇ : (2♣), or 1♣ : (2◇)... Here a double shows both majors, at least 4-4, perhaps 5-4, 5-5 or 6-4. A major suit bid at the 1-level need not be longer than 4 cards and promises just 6 points or more. A major suit response at the 2-level, however, would promise a 5-card or longer suit and 10 points or more, obviously forcing.

(b) Minor-Major or Major-Minor : Where only one major suit has been bid so far, the negative double promises at least 4 cards in the other major. For example, 1♣ : (1♠) : Double shows at least 4 hearts or, again, 1♡ : (2♣) : Double shows at least 4 spades. If partner opens with a minor suit and they intervene with 1♡, the double now promises precisely *four* spades while a response of 1♠ would show at least *five* spades.

(c) Major-Major : If partner has opened in one major and they intervene with the other major, the double now shows *both* minors, at least 4-4 but it could be 5-4, 5-5 or 6-4. The negative double would promise 6 points or more while a change of suit by responder at the 2-level or higher would promise 10 points or more. Suppose you picked up a hand like this : ♠ 43   ♡ 4   ◇ K8754   ♣ AJ642 and the bidding started with 1♠ from partner and 2♡ on your right. Instead of fearing interference, you would welcome it here if you were using negative doubles, since the double allows you to express the nature and strength of the hand quite accurately whereas without the interference you would have no descriptive response.

Subsequent bidding after a negative double : Where responder's negative double has promised a specific major, opener rebids as though the responder had bid that major at the 1-level. For example, if the bidding had started 1♣ : (1♠) : Double ... the opener would continue as though the responder had replied 1♡. Thus, if fourth player passes and opener rebids 3♡, it would be equivalent to an auction of 1♣ : 1♡, 3♡ without interference.

A negative double followed by a change of suit by responder implies at least a 5-card suit. In this case, responder would also be implying at most 9 HCP, since with 11 or more points and a 5-card or longer suit, the responder would have been strong enough to bid the suit at once. So, for example, if opener starts with 1♣ and responder doubles a 1♠ overcall and over opener's 2♣ rebid, responder rebids 2♡, responder is showing 5 or more hearts and 6-9 points only, for with more than that, the original response would have been 2♡.

EXAMPLE HANDS USING THE NEGATIVE DOUBLE

How should the following hands be bid? West is the dealer on each hand and North intervenes with 1♠ on each hand. No other opposition bidding.

HAND 1

WEST	EAST
♠ 8 4	♠ 9 5 2
♡ K 7 6	♡ A J 5 3
◇ A 4	◇ J 10 9 3
♣ A Q 7 4 3 2	♣ J 6

After 1♣ by West, 1♠ overall by North, East doubles to show 4 hearts and 6 or more points. West, unable to support hearts or rebid no-trumps, would rebid 2♣ to show a minimum opening with a long club suit. With a minimum double, East passes.

HAND 2

WEST	EAST
♠ A 8	♠ 3 2
♡ 6 4	♡ Q J 10 9 3 2
◇ K Q 7 6 5	◇ 8 4
♣ K J 3 2	♣ A 5 4

After 1◇ by West, 1♠ overcall by North, East is too weak to bid 2♡ (at least 10 points needed) and doubles (showing only 6 points or more with at least 4 hearts). West rebids 2♣ and East removes to 2♡, confirming 5 or more hearts, 6-9 points. West passes.

HAND 3

WEST	EAST
♠ A 9 3 2	♠ 6 5
♡ K 9 8 4	♡ A 6 3 2
◇ Q	◇ A J 3 2
♣ A 6 4 3	♣ K 8 7

After 1♣ by West, 1♠ overcall by North, East has enough to bid a game, but is not sure of the best game. East doubles and awaits further information. West bids 2♡ to show four hearts but with only a minimum opening. This is enough to enable East to bid 4♡.

HAND 4

WEST	EAST
♠ 7 3	♠ A 10
♡ A 8	♡ K 9 7 3
◇ A 9 8 7 3 2	◇ K Q 4
♣ A 8 6	♣ J 4 3 2

After 1◇ by West, 1♠ overcall by North, East has enough for game, but should double, to try for hearts, rather than bid no-trumps at once. When West rebids 2◇, a minimum opening with long diamonds, East rebids 3NT since there is no fit in hearts.

HAND 5

WEST	EAST
♠ 8	♠ 7 6 2
♡ A Q 7 2	♡ K 9 5 3
◇ K Q 3	◇ A 7 6 4
♣ A Q J 8 4	♣ 6 5

After 1♣ by West, 1♠ overcall by North, East doubles to show 4 hearts and 6 or more points. West is worth 21 points in support of hearts, (3 for the singleton) and therefore rebids 4♡. A fringe benefit of the negative double is that the strong hand is often declarer.

APPENDIX 6 : BRIDGE MYTHS AND FALLACIES

The following common fallacies may contain a grain of truth or logic but their value is diminished when they are treated as absolute, unfailing, universal principles. At best, the following are reasonable guides which should be discarded when the circumstances warrant.

(1) "Always lead top of partner's suit" : No, no, a thousand times no. This approach can cost you tricks in defense time after time. Lead top only from a doubleton or from a sequence or from three cards headed by two touching honors, *but* lead bottom from three or four to an honor and middle from three with no honor. See Appendix 4 and also Hand 29 on page 76.

(2) "Always return your partner's lead" : This has more merit but the rule is far too wide. It is often best to return your partner's lead but there are many situations where you are able to recognise the need for a switch (e.g. see Hands 31 and 32 on page 77). Keep in mind the number of tricks needed to defeat the contract and, unless a passive defense is clearly indicated, avoid continuing suits which are known to be futile for beating the contract.

(3) "Never lead from a king" : To lead from a king-high holding is not an especially attractive lead but there are also far worse combinations. It is usually more dangerous to lead away from a suit headed by the queen or by the jack and far worse in a trump contract to lead from a suit headed by the ace without the king as well. The popular leads of J-x or Q-x in an unbid suit are also far more dangerous than leading from a king. They would be reasonable if partner had bid the suit but other than that they should be shunned. Leading from a king is acceptable when you judge that the other possibilities are riskier.

(4) "Always cover an honor with an honor" : Rubbish. It is correct to cover an honor with an honor if it will promote cards in your hand or if it might promote winners in partner's hand. In the trump suit in particular, it is usually wrong to cover an honor unless partner has length in trumps.

(5) " Lead through strength and up to weakness" : This has some sense behind it but card-reading and counting provide better guides for the defense. Leading through strength does not apply to the opening lead (it is rarely best to lead dummy's bid suit) and in the middle game, the rule refers to short suits (doubletons or tripletons). It is normally not in your best interests to attack dummy's or declarer's long side suit.

(6) "Eight ever, nine never" : When missing the queen of a long suit, proper technique is to finesse for it if you have 8 cards together and to play the ace and king, hoping the queen will drop, when you have 9 cards. When playing a complete hand, however, there can be many other considerations.

APPENDIX 7 : ETHICS AND ETIQUETTE

Bridge enjoys immense popularity partly because of the high standards of ethics and etiquette which are observed by the players who are expected to conduct themselves in a highly civilised manner. Violations of proper etiquette are quite common from inexperienced players, either through ignorance or inadvertence. A well-mannered opponent who is the victim of a violation by such a novice player will, if comment is considered necessary, be at pains to make it clear that the comment is intended to be helpful and will never make a newcomer feel ill-at-ease.

Bridge is an extremely ethical game. All good players strive to ensure that their bridge ethics are impeccable and no more serious charge, other than outright cheating, can be made than to accuse a player of bad ethics. Unlike poker in which all sorts of mannerisms, misleading statements and bluff tactics are part and parcel of the game, bridge is played with a "poker-face"! Beginners are, of course, excused for their lapses and in social games nobody minds very much, but in serious competition your bridge demeanour must be beyond reproach.

When you are dummy, it is poor form to look at either opponent's hand or at declarer's. If you do, you lose your rights as dummy. Do not stand behind declarer to see how you would play the contract. In tournament bridge, do not discuss the previous hand with your partner if there is still another hand to be played. After the play of a hand is over, do not take an opponent's cards and look at them without asking permission. As a kibitzer (onlooker), try to watch only one hand and above all, do not make any facial expressions during a hand and do not comment or talk during or even between hands. If the players want the benefit of your views, they will ask for them.

Conversation at the table in serious games is generally unwelcome. Post-mortems after each hand, if limited, can be useful as long as they seek to be constructive, but it is preferable to keep all post-mortems until after the session is over and you can go over the score-sheets with your partner at your leisure rather than at a time when you should be conserving your energies to do battle at the next table. It is in extremely poor taste to abuse or criticise partner or an opponent. Experienced players should go out of their way to make novice players feel at ease, so that they will view bridge as a pleasant recreation, not a battleground. Never try to 'teach' anyone at the table. Never let a harsh word pass your lips and you will be a sought-after rather than a shunned partner. Prefer to say too little than too much. If partner has bid or played the hand like an idiot, say "bad luck" and leave it at that. Do not harp on past errors.

Use only the proper language of bridge. The correct expression when not making a bid is "Pass". Do not use "No bid". Stick to "Pass" but if you happen to use "No bid", use that all the time and do not switch back and forth between "Pass" and "No bid". Do not say "Content", "Okay", "By me". Do not say "I'll double one heart" — just say "Double". Do not say "Spade" when you mean "One Spade".

Never vary the intonation in your bidding — softly on weak hands, loudly on good ones. Never put a question mark at the end of your bid to make sure that partner understands that your 4NT is Blackwood or that your double is for takeout. That would be quite atrocious. You are supposed to convey messages to partner by what you bid, not by the way you bid it. Frowns, scowls, smiles, raised eyebrows, etc., are out. You are not to adopt the tongue-in-cheek remark made by the legendary Groucho Marx to his partners, "Don't bother to signal. If you like my leads, just smile. I'll understand."

If your partner has a good sense of humor, you may be able to make clever remarks such as: "When did you learn to play? I know, this afternoon, but what time this afternoon?", or in reply to "How should I have played that hand?" "Under an assumed name", or in reply to "How did I play that hand?" "Like a millionaire", or in reply to "Could I have done any better?", "I suppose double dummy you could have gone one more down", or in reply to "Did I play that all right?" "Well, you didn't knock the coffee over" but in general, bridge players are a proud lot with sensitive egos. Politeness and courtesy should be your watchword at the bridge table as in other areas in life.

Long pausing before bidding is also to be avoided; for example, the pause followed by "Pass" tells everyone that you have 11-12 points, not quite good enough to open. Make all your bids at the same pace if you can. Sometimes, of course, you will have a serious problem which takes you some time to resolve, but where this happens the obligation falls on the partner of the 'trancer' who must never take advantage of the information received from the pause. Play your cards as a defender always at the same speed if possible. Fumbling or hesitating *with the intention of deceiving declarer* is cheating. You must not try to mislead opponents by your manner.

In tournament bridge, if you are ever in doubt as to the correct procedure, always call the Tournament Director. Do not let other players tell you what the correct laws are. They are wrong more often than not. Nobody familiar with the tournament scene minds the director being called. It is not considered a slight, an insult, or a rebuff to the opposition.

Above all, remember that bridge is primarily a game and is meant to be enjoyed. Make sure it is also enjoyable for the other players at your table.

APPENDIX 8 : TOURNAMENT BRIDGE

The main kinds of competitive bridge are pairs events and teams events. Bridge is played internationally and in each odd-numbered year there are World Teams Championships (the Bermuda Bowl for open championships, the Venice Cup for women's championships) in which 8-10 teams representing different geographical zones compete. Every four years, there is a Bridge Olympiad in which a far greater number of teams compete. In recent years, more than sixty countries have been represented at these Olympiads. In the other even-numbered years there are the World Pairs Championships (open pairs, women's pairs, mixed pairs) as well as the World Open Teams (for the Rosenblum Cup). Each country conducts national championships and many tournaments of lower status. In addition, there are tournaments to select the players who will represent their country. Some countries and most clubs conduct an Individual Championship once a year. In pairs and teams events, you keep the same partner for each session and usually throughout the event. In an Individual, each competitor plays with every other competitor for one, two or three deals, so that these are not considered serious events and a calm temperament is a prerequisite to surviving an Individual.

In general, pairs events are more common than any other type of event. The advantage of tournament bridge is that the element of having good cards or bad cards is reduced to a minimum, since all players play exactly the same deals. Another advantage is that you can compete against the top players merely by playing in the same tournament. In few other sports could a novice play against a world champion in a tournament. Tournament bridge also improves your game, since the hand records are available to check afterwards where you may have gone wrong.

There are some differences between tournament bridge and ordinary ('rubber') bridge in regard to technicalities and strategy. Except at the first table, you will not shuffle and deal the cards. The cards come to you in a tray, called a 'board' and you must put the cards back in the correct slot after the board has been played. The board is marked N, E, S, and W, and must be placed properly on the table; the board also states which side is vulnerable and who is the dealer. During the play, the cards are not thrown into the middle of the table, but each player, including dummy, keeps the cards in front of them, turning them face down after the trick has been completed. You may examine the trick just played only while your card remains face up. Each card is placed so as to point in the direction of the side that wins the trick. After the hand is over, you can see at a glance how many tricks have been won and how many have been lost.

Each board in tournament bridge is scored independently. In rubber bridge if you make a partscore you have an advantage for the next hand, but in tournament bridge you do not carry forward partscores. You enter the score for the hand just played, and on the next board, both sides start from zero again.

As each deal is totally unrelated to what happened on the previous deal, there are significant scoring differences in tournament bridge :

(1) Honors do not count (unless otherwise stated by the tournament rules).
(2) For bidding and making a partscore, add 50 to the trick total.
(3) For bidding and making a game, not vulnerable, add 300 to the trick total.
(4) For bidding and making a game, vulnerable, add 500 to the trick total.
(5) The fourth and subsequent undertricks doubled and not vulnerable are 300.

The result you obtain on the board is entered on the 'travelling score sheet' at the back of the board. You may not look at that until the hand is over, since it contains a record of the hand and also how other pairs fared on the board. Your score on each board is compared with the scores of every other pair that played the board. If you are sitting North-South, then your real opponents are all the other North-South pairs competing, not the particular pair you play each time. On each board, a certain number of match-points is awarded (usually one less than the number of pairs who play the board). If 15 pairs play a board, the best score receives 14 match-points, a 'top', the next best score receives 13 match-points and so on down to the worst score which receives 0 match-points, a 'bottom'. An average score would receive 7 match-points. The scoring is done once for the N-S pairs and then for the E-W pairs. Obviously, if a N-S pair scores a top, the corresponding E-W pair against whom they played the board gets a bottom. Each pair's points over all the boards are totalled and the pair with the highest number of match-points wins.

Tactics in pairs events differ from those in rubber bridge. Careful declarer play and defense are the order of the day. Every overtrick and every undertrick could be vital . . . they make the difference between good scores and bad scores. In rubber bridge, declarer's aim is almost always to make the contract and the defense's aim is to defeat it . . . at pairs, the aim is to obtain the best possible score which may mean from declarer's viewpoint that making the contract is a secondary consideration while from the defenders' viewpoint, the possibility of giving away an overtrick in trying to defeat the contract may be unwarranted.

Being extremely competitive in the bidding is essential. Almost always force the opposition to the three-level on partscore deals. Be quick to re-open the bidding if they stop at a very low level in a suit. . In pairs events, re-opening the bidding occurs ten times more often than at rubber bridge.

Minor suit contracts, especially at the game zone, should be avoided. Prefer 3NT to 5♣ or 5♢, even if 3NT is riskier, since making an overtrick in 3NT scores more than a minor suit game. On the other hand, it is not necessary to bid close games or close slams. The reward for success is not so great in pairs events as to justify 24 point games or 31 point slams. You should be in game or in slam if it has a 50% or better chance. If less, you will score better by staying out of it.

What counts at duplicate pairs is how often a certain strategy will work for you, not the size of the result. If a certain action scores 50 extra points 8 times out of 10, but loses 500 twice, it is sensible at duplicate but ridiculous at rubber bridge. Penalty doubles are far more frequent at pairs since players are anxious to improve their score. The rule about a two-trick safety margin is frequently disregarded since one down, doubled, vulnerable, may be a top-score while one down, undoubled, vulnerable, may be below average.

Safety plays which involve sacrificing a trick to ensure the contract almost never apply in pairs, unless the contract you have reached is an unbelievably good one.

In the tournament world you will run up against a remarkable number and variety of systems and conventions and gradually you will come to recognise them. The more important ones have been listed in Appendix 10. A most important point to remember is that a bidding system is not some secret between you and your partner. You and your partner are not allowed to have any secret understanding about your bids. That is *cheating*. A bidding system is not a secret code. The opponents are entitled to know as much about what the bidding means as you or your partner. If they ask you what you understand by a certain bid of your partner's, you must tell them truthfully. Of course, your partner's bid may be meaningless and if you cannot understand it, all you can do is to be honest and tell the opposition that you do not know what partner's bid means.

Similarly, if you do not understand the opposition's bidding, you are entitled to ask. When it is your turn to bid but before you make your bid, you ask the partner of the bidder "What do you understand by that bid?" You may ask during the auction or after the auction has ended, when it is your turn to play. Unless it affects your making a bid, prefer to wait until the auction is over. After all, the opposition might not understand their bidding either and when you ask, they may well realise their mistake.

If an irregularity occurs at the table, do not be dismayed if the director is summoned. That is a normal part of the game and it is the director's job to keep the tournament running smoothly and to sort out any irregularities.

APPENDIX 9 : HOW TO IMPROVE YOUR GAME

After you have been playing for some time, the following suggestions may assist you in your desire to improve :

(a) Play rubber bridge for as high stakes as you can afford with players who are better than you. This will cost you money but the experience is invaluable for you will learn why they are better than you. You will scarcely improve, although you will undoubtedly enjoy your game, if you are better than the players with whom you are playing.

(b) Kibitz (watch) the best players in action. There are tournaments continually in progress in which top-flight players are playing. It usually costs you nothing to go along and watch experts play. Very few experts object to being watched. On the contrary it boosts their ego, and they may even explain why they made a certain bid or a certain play. To obtain the most benefit from such kibitzing, you should watch one player exclusively and try to decide what you would bid and play if you had the same cards. Then you can compare your solution with what the expert does in practice. If there is a startling discrepancy, you might ask for guidance. Very few experts mind explaining to those who are seeking to learn.

(c) Read some bridge books. There are a few excellent books on bidding and quite a number on the play of the cards. Unfortunately there are also quite a few which are somewhat less than excellent. Ask an expert or a good bridge teacher for advice about what books you should be reading. At the early stages, books on card play are the better investment.

There is some controversy whether bridge players are born or are made. It used to be the case that the natural player had a considerable edge over those who found bridge hard work. However, even the natural players now have to do a fair amount of book-work to keep up with technical advances. Flair is certainly a help, but expert technique is an asset that can be acquired.

(d) Play tournament bridge as often as you are able. Play with a partner who is better than you (if that is possible). Take particular notice of what happens when you come up against expert pairs.

(e) Take advanced lessons from the best teachers available.

(f) Keep up to date with bridge magazines. There are excellent magazines in the USA as well as overseas magazine. Seek the advice of a top player.

What is fascinating about bridge is that it can be enjoyed at all levels, but you will find that the better you play, the more you enjoy it.

APPENDIX 10 : POPULAR CONVENTIONS & SYSTEMS

The following brief descriptions outline some of the more popular conventions and systems that you may come across, particularly in tournament bridge. Before you adopt any of them, you should already be playing a sound game and, of course, you should have discussed them fully with your partner first.

1. Stayman 2♣ over a 1NT opening: This is an artificial enquiry by the responder, asking whether the opener holds a 4-card major. It is discussed in this book on page 93. This convention is highly recommended, is used almost universally and is vital for tournament players.

2. Stayman 3♣ over a 2NT opening: This is likewise set out in Appendix 1 on page 93 and is also highly recommended. It is superior to the Baron 3♣ convention (which after a 2NT opening asks the opener to bid 4-card suits up-the-line), since Stayman allows the strong hand to remain declarer more frequently and copes easily with 5-4 patterns as well as finding 4-4 fits.

3. Blackwood 4NT asking for aces: This invaluable convention is almost universally played and is discussed in Chapter 8, pages 58-59.

4. Gerber 4♣ asking for aces: This convention asks for aces and kings in a manner similar to Blackwood 4NT except that the enquiry bid is 4♣ and the replies are: 4◇ = 0 or 4; 4♡ = 1; 4♠ = 2; 4NT = 3. After the answer to 4♣, the ask for kings is initiated by 5♣. Gerber 4♣ is rarely used by expert partnerships because it conflicts with Cuebidding.

5. Cuebidding: This is a method of slam bidding in which partners tell each other which aces and kings are held as opposed to how many are held (which is the answer to 4NT Blackwood or 4♣ Gerber). It is a superior slam-bidding method and is used widely among expert partnerships.

6. 5NT Grand Slam Force: This is an asking bid about the trump suit but it does not apply if 4NT Blackwood was used. 4NT Blackwood followed by 5NT is an asking bid for kings (see page 59), but a jump to 5NT or a bid of 5NT in a cuebidding sequence asks partner about the A, K and Q of trumps. There are many versions of the 5NT Trump Ask. A simple and effective one is for partner to answer in the same way Blackwood 4NT would be answered. Thus, 6♣ = 0; 6◇ = 1; 6♡ = 2; 6♠ = 3. The difference is that the question is not about aces but about the A, K and Q of trumps. Until you have a regular partnership and wish to adopt something more complex, this variation of the 5NT Trump Ask will function efficiently and it has the virtue of being easy to remember.

7. Weak No-Trumps: Not everyone uses the same point range for the 1NT opening. The most common range for the weak 1NT is 12-14, but occasionally the 13-15 range is used, as in the Precision system.

8. Strong No-Trumps: The range for the strong no-trump is 16-18 points, but 15-17 or 15-18 point ranges are also popular.

9. Weak Twos: This refers to the approach of opening 2♡ and 2♠ (and occasionally 2♢ as well) on weak hands of 6-10 HCP with a strong 6-card suit. They are very popular in tournament bridge since they arise far more often than the super-strong two openings. They are both pre-emptive and constructive and the disciplined approach is not to open a weak two with a void or two singletons in the hand or with a 4-card major. Pairs using weak twos open super-strong hands with artificial bids of 2♣ or 2♢ (see page 56).

10. Benjamin Twos: This refers to a popular treatment for two-openings in which 2♡ and 2♠ are weak twos, 2♢ is a force to game based on about 23 HCP or better and 2♣ is a strong bid but not forcing to game. 2♢ and 2♣ are both artificial openings, of course, and partner's negative reply is the next suit up. A positive reply to 2♣ is forcing to game and a positive reply to 2♢ strongly suggests slam prospects. The 2♣ opening is generally based on a strong one-suiter of around 19-22 points (8½-9½ playing tricks) or a two-suiter around the 21-22 point mark. The treatment is highly attractive because it allows a partnership to bid both weak hands and strong hands more accurately than other systems of opening two-bids.

11. Weak Jump-Overcalls: A treatment in which a single jump-overcall is played as a weak bid, around 6-10 HCP and a 6-card or longer suit. The method is popular in tournament bridge but not at rubber bridge.

12. Transfer Bids: A method in which a player bids the suit below the actual suit held, so that partner can bid the real suit. It is used normally only after a 1NT or 2NT opening and has many advantages over standard methods. It frequently enables the stronger hand to become declarer in suit contracts and enables a partnership to bid a far vaster range of hands more precisely than standard methods permit.

13. Precision System, Schenken, Big Club: Systems in which the 1♣ opening bid shows a powerful hand, usually around 16 or 17 points or more. As a consequence, opening bids other than the artificial 1♣ are limited in strength to less than the requirements for 1♣.

14. Underleading Honors: A system of opening leads where a player leads the second card in a sequence rather than the standard top of sequence.

APPENDIX 11

THE MECHANICS AND RULES OF BRIDGE — HOW THE GAME IS PLAYED

This appendix will help to dispel any doubts you might have about the rules or procedure when playing bridge.

Bridge is a game for four players, playing in two partnerships. It represents a head-to-head battle — your side against their side. Partners sit opposite each other. Partnerships are chosen by agreement or by lot. The common method is for each player to choose a card from the pack fanned out face down, with the players selecting the two highest cards as one partnership against the players selecting the two lowest cards.

THE BRIDGE PACK

A regular pack of 52 cards is used and there are no jokers and no cards of any exceptional rank or function (unlike 500 where jacks have a special role, or Canasta where 2s are jokers).

There are four suits :

♠ SPADES — ♡ HEARTS — ◇ DIAMONDS — ♣ CLUBS

Each suit consists of thirteen cards which in order of rank are: A, K, Q, J, 10, 9, 8, 7, 6, 5, 4, 3, 2. An ace beats a king, a king beats a queen, a queen beats a jack, a jack beats a ten and so on. The top five cards in each suit, namely the A, K, Q, J and 10, are known as the honor cards or honors.

The suits also have a ranking order: CLUBS (♣) is the *lowest* suit, then come DIAMONDS (◇) and HEARTS (♡) to the highest ranking suit, SPADES (♠). NO-TRUMPS ranks higher than any suit. The order of the suits — C, D, H, S — is no accident. They are in alphabetical order.

When selecting partnerships, if two cards of the same rank are chosen (e.g. two eights) and the tie needs to be broken, it is decided by suit order (e.g. the ◇ 8 would outrank the ♣8).

DEALING

The player who drew the highest card is the dealer on the first hand and has the right to choose seats and the pack of cards with which to deal. The next dealer will be the person on the left of the previous dealer and so on, in clockwise rotation.

The cards are shuffled by the person on the dealer's left. The dealer passes the pack across the table to the person on the dealer's right to be cut. The dealer then deals the cards, one at a time, face down, in clockwise direction, starting with the player on the left, until all 52 cards are dealt, 13 each.

It is usual to leave your cards face down until the dealer has finished dealing. A misdeal may be corrected if the players have not seen their cards. While the dealer is dealing, the partner of the dealer is shuffling the other pack in preparation for the next deal. Two packs are used in order to speed up the game. After the shuffling is finished the cards are put down on the shuffler's right, ready for the next dealer to pick up.

THE START OF PLAY

When you pick up your 13 cards, you sort them into suits. It is normal to separate the red suits and black suits so that you can easily see where one suit ends and the next suit begins.

The bidding starts with the dealer. After the bidding period is over, the side that has bid higher wins the right to play the hand. One member of this side, called the declarer, plays the hand while the opponents defend the hand. The person on the left of the declarer makes the opening lead. The partner of the declarer, called the dummy, now puts all thirteen cards face up on the table and arranged in suits. The dummy takes no further part in the play, declarer playing both hands. Each player can see 26 cards, the 13 in hand plus the 13 in dummy.

Declarer plays one of the cards from dummy, then the third player plays a card and so does declarer. The four cards now face up on the table are called a *trick*. A trick always consists of four cards played in clockwise sequence, one from each hand.

Each deal in bridge is a battle over thirteen tricks, declarer trying to win as many as nominated in the bidding, while the defenders try to win enough tricks to defeat declarer. A trick is won by the highest card played. The player who wins the trick gathers the four cards together, puts them face down neatly and then leads to the next trick, and so on until all thirteen tricks have been played. (In tournament bridge, called 'duplicate', the cards are not gathered together. The players keeps their own cards in front of them.)

FOLLOWING SUIT

The player who plays the highest ranking card *of the suit led* wins the trick. If two or more cards of the same rank are played to one trick, who wins then? The basic rule of play is: *YOU MUST FOLLOW SUIT,* i.e. you must play a card of the same suit as the suit led. If hearts are led, then you must play a heart if you have one and the trick is won by the highest heart played, so that if the two of hearts is led, and the other cards on the trick are the ten of hearts, the queen of spades and the ace of clubs, the trick is won by the ten of hearts. If you are unable to follow suit, you may play any other card at all, but remember it is the highest card of the first led suit which wins. If the king of spades is led, it will do you no good to play the ace of clubs — only the ace of spades beats the king of spades.

TRUMPS

There is one exception to this. Where one of the four suits is, in the bidding, made the *trump* suit, then any card in the trump suit is higher than any card, even an ace, in one of the other suits. So, if hearts are trumps, the two of hearts would beat the ace of clubs even when clubs are led. But, first and foremost, you must follow suit. Only when you are out of a suit can you beat a high card of another suit with a trump.

If you are unable to follow suit, you are allowed to trump, *but it is not obligatory.* You may choose to discard and if, for example, partner has already won the trick, it may be foolish to trump partner's winner.

A trick that does not contain a trump is won by the highest card in the suit led. A trick that contains a trump is won by the highest trump in the trick. If you fail to follow suit when able to do so, you have 'revoked' (or 'reneged'). The penalty for a revoke is to transfer one or two tricks to the other side, one trick if you do not win the revoking trick, two tricks if you do win the revoking trick.

THE BIDDING

The play is preceded by the bidding, also called 'the auction'. Just as in an auction an item goes to the highest bidder, so in the bridge auction each side tries to outbid the other for the right to be declarer and play the hand.

The dealer makes the first bid, then the player on dealer's left and so on in clockwise rotation. Each player may decline to bid (say "Pass") or make a bid. A player who has previously passed may still make a bid later in the auction. A bid consists of a number (1, 2, 3, 4, 5, 6 or 7) followed by a suit or no-trumps, e.g. two spades, three hearts, four no-trumps, seven diamonds. 'No-Trumps' means that there is to be no trump suit on the deal.

Whenever a bid is made, the bidder is stating the number of tricks *above six* intended to be won in the play. The minimum number of tricks that you may contract for is seven. A bid of 1 Club contracts to make seven tricks with clubs as trumps. The number in the bid is the number of tricks to be won *over and above six tricks.* (Six tricks is not even halfway and you have to bid for more than half the tricks.) The final bid is the 'contract'.

If all players pass without a bid on the first round, there is no play, there is no score, the cards are thrown in and the next dealer deals a new hand. When a player makes a bid on the first round, the auction has started and will be won by the side that bids higher. The auction continues, with each player making a bid or passing, and concludes as soon as a bid is followed by three passes. The side that bids higher sets the trump suit (or no-trumps) and the number of tricks to be won in the play; this is set by the final bid and the member of the side who first bid the trump suit (or no-trumps) is the declarer.

After a bid, any player in turn may make a *higher* bid. A bid is higher than a previous bid if it is a larger number than the previous bid, or the same number but in a higher ranking denomination. The order of ranking is:

> NO-TRUMPS
> SPADES
> HEARTS
> DIAMONDS
> CLUBS

A bid of 1 Heart is higher than a bid of 1 Club. If you want to bid clubs and the previous bid was 2 Spades, you would have to bid 3 Clubs (or 4 Clubs or 5 Clubs or higher). 2 Clubs would not be higher than 2 Spades.

GAME AND RUBBER

A rubber of bridge is over when one side wins two games. A game is won by scoring 100 or more points when declarer.

It is vital to understand how the game is scored, for this affects both the bidding and the play. Your aim is to score more points than the opposition. You may score points : (1) by bidding and making a contract as declarer (2) by defeating the opponents at their contract (3) by earning bonus points.

Some points are written above the line, some below the line on the score-sheet. When adding up the totals, all points count equally, but points below the line are especially valuable, since these are the only points that count towards game. *Only the declarer side can score points for game.* That is the incentive for bidding higher than the opponents. *You score points below the line by bidding and making a contract,* according to this table :

NO-TRUMPS	40 points for the first trick (over six),
(NT)	30 for each subsequent trick.
♠ SPADES	30 points for each trick (over six) — *major suit.*
♡ HEARTS	30 points for each trick (over six) — *major suit.*
◇ DIAMONDS	20 points for each trick (over six) — *minor suit.*
♣ CLUBS	20 points for each trick (over six) — *minor suit.*

Since game is 100 points or more, it takes a bid of 5 Clubs or 5 Diamonds to make game in the minors, while a bid of 4 Hearts or 4 Spades or more will score game in the majors. In no-trumps, a bid of 3NT will score a game.

The declaring side gets credit not for the tricks won but only for the tricks bid and then won. So if 4♡ is bid, and declarer makes 9 tricks, declarer does not get credit for 9 tricks but suffers a penalty for failing to make the contract by one trick. Thus accuracy in bidding distinguishes contract bridge from auction bridge (where you are given credit for what you make, even if you did not bid it) and becomes the single most important element in the game's winning strategy.

If declarer makes more tricks than the contract calls for, the extra tricks ('overtricks') are not lost, but are scored as bonuses *above the line.*

Only points scored by winning the actual number of tricks of the contract are written below the line and only points below the line count towards winning games and the rubber.

A score below the line of less than 100 is called a *partscore.* You may combine two or more partscores to score the 100 points for game. You cannot carry forward any points over and above 100 to the next game. After one side scores a game, a line is drawn across both columns and both sides start again from zero towards the next game. So, if you have a partscore but the enemy score a game before you have been able to convert your partscore into a game, you have to start from zero for the next game ... they have *underlined* you.

DOUBLES AND REDOUBLES

In the bidding, any player may at his turn double a bid made by an opponent. Say 'Double'. If there is no further bidding, the double increases the rewards for success and the penalties for failure. After a double, the other side may redouble (say 'Redouble'), increasing the rewards and penalties further.

Any double or redouble is cancelled by a bid, but there may be further doubles and redoubles of later bids. 1♠ making 7 tricks scores 30 below the line, but 1♠ doubled and redoubled making 7 tricks scores 120 below the line (and game!), plus 50 bonus points for making a doubled contract ('for the insult').

OTHER SCORING

There is a complete scoring table on the inside front cover to which you can refer if in doubt. *You should know the trick value of each suit and no-trumps* and you should also know some of the more common scores which go above the line, but the rest of the scoring can be learned gradually, as you play.

A side that has scored one game is said to be vulnerable and needs only one more game to complete the rubber. Penalties are more severe for failing to make a contract when vulnerable than when not vulnerable.

When one side fails to make its contract, the other side scores 50 points per undertrick if declarer is not vulnerable and 100 points per undertrick if declarer is vulnerable. These and all other bonus points go above the line. If the final contract was doubled or redoubled, the penalties are more severe (see the scoring table, inside front cover). Note that penalties are the same whatever the contract is. One down in 2♡ is the same as one down in 7NT.

You score bonus points for finishing the rubber (700 for 2 games to 0 or 500 for 2 games to 1), for making overtricks in a doubled or redoubled contract (see scoring table) and also for holding 'honors'. The honor cards are the A, K, Q, J and 10, and you score 150 points for all 5 trump honors in one hand, 100 points for any 4 of the 5 trump honors in one hand, or 150 points for 4 aces in one hand, but only if the contract is no-trumps.

Bonuses for honors are scored whether or not the contract is made. Honors may be held by declarer, dummy or either defender. In order not to tell the opposition what cards you hold, honors are usually claimed after the hand has been played. Honors are not scored when playing duplicate.

A contract of six (12 tricks) is called a small slam and if you *bid and make* a small slam, you score above the line :

500 points if not vulnerable, 750 points if vulnerable.

A contract of seven (13 tricks) is called a grand slam, and if you *bid and make* a grand slam, you score above the line :

1000 points if not vulnerable, 1500 points if vulnerable.

After deducting the losers' total from the winners' total, the net balance is rounded off to the nearest 100 (50 at the end of a score goes down, not up). The score for the rubber is entered next to each player's name on a tally card and the next rubber is then started, either with the same partnerships or by drawing again for new partners. Bridge may be played with or without stakes. The amount of the stakes will be by agreement among the players. The stakes are usually stipulated at so much per hundred points, e.g. ten cents a hundred.

GLOSSARY AND INDEX

ANSWERS TO EXERCISES AND BIDDING PRACTICE

Page   Answers

13   **Exercise 1 :**   1. Unbalanced   2. Unbalanced   3. Semi-balanced
     4. Balanced   5. Balanced   6. Balanced   7. Unbalanced   8. Unbalanced

Exercise 2 :	**A**	**B**	**C**	**D**
Hand 1	13	Semi-balanced	5-4-2-2	2-suiter
Hand 2	14	Balanced	4-4-3-2	2-suiter
Hand 3	14	Balanced	4-3-3-3	1-suiter
Hand 4	13	Unbalanced	5-5-2-1	2-suiter
Hand 5	11	Semi-balanced	6-3-2-2	1-suiter
Hand 6	12	Unbalanced	6-5-2-0	2-suiter
Hand 7	14	Unbalanced	4-4-4-1	3-suiter
Hand 8	13	Unbalanced	6-4-3-0	2-suiter

19   1. One club   2. One heart   3. Pass   4. One heart   5. One spade.
     Start with the higher ranking suit with 5-5 patterns.   6. One spade
     7. One heart   8. One diamond. Start with the longer suit even if
     you have a 5-card major as well.   9. Pass. With 12 hcp and a 4-3-3-3
     pattern it is better to pass in first or second seat. In third or fourth
     seat, you may open with these values and even with less if you have
     a strong suit.   10. One diamond   11. One club   12. One club.
     With 3-3 in the minors, open one club regardless of the suit quality.
     13. One club   14. One club   15. One diamond. With 4-4 in the
     minors, open one diamond.   16. One diamond   17. One diamond
     18. One club   19. One diamond. 4-4 minors.   20. One diamond
     21. Pass   22. One spade. 11 hcp is enough if you have a 6-card suit
     or two 5-card suits.   23. One spade   24. One club   25. One diamond.
     With no 5-card suit, open the longer minor.   26. One club. Longer
     minor.   27. One diamond. 4-4 minors.   28. One club. 3-3 minors.

23   **Exercise A :**   1. 1NT. You do not need a stopper in every suit to
     open 1NT.   2. 1NT. The 5-3-3-2 is a balanced shape. If the 5-card
     suit is a minor, prefer the no-trump opening if the point count is right.
     3. One spade. Prefer the 5-card major to 1NT.   4. One diamond.
     Beyond 1NT and below 2NT, start with a suit opening.
     Exercise B :   1. 3NT.   2. Pass. With 16-18 opposite, there cannot
     be 26 points together.   3. 2NT.   4. 3NT. The 5-3-3-2 is balanced.
     Partnership Bidding Practice :   1. Pass : 1NT, Pass
     2. 1NT : 2NT, 3NT   3. Pass : 1NT, 3NT. West has 10 points,
     counting one for the 5-card suit.   4. 1NT : 2NT, Pass. 2NT shows
     8-9 points, but with only 16, opener should pass 2NT. Even that

might fail.   5. Pass: 1NT, 2NT: 3NT. Opener with 17-18 should
accept the 2NT invitation.   6. 1NT: Pass   7. 1NT: Pass. Seven
points in a balanced hand is not enough to make a move towards
game.   8. Pass : 1NT, 3NT. The 5-3-3-2 is a balanced pattern.

28   **(a)**   1. One diamond. Longest suit first.   2. One heart. Up-the-line
with 4-card suits.   3. One spade   4. One spade. Show a major
rather than support a minor.   5. One heart. There is no suit quality
requirement when bidding a 4-card suit.   6. One diamond. Longer
suit first.   7. One heart. Even a 4-card major should be shown
before showing 5-card or better support.   8. Pass. Too weak to
reply even if you do not like the suit partner opened.

(b)   1. One spade. Show even a weak major before supporting a minor.
2. One heart   3. One spade   4. One spade   5. One heart   6. One
spade. Technically the major suit should be shown before raising the
diamonds. However, five diamonds would be a sensible, practical bid.
7. One heart. Too weak for two clubs (showing 10 or more points).
8. Pass.

(c)   1. One spade. Too weak for two diamonds.   2. Two hearts.
If the values allow, support a major rather than change suit.
3. One spade.   4. One spade   5. Two hearts   6. One spade. Very
close between this and two diamonds.   7. Two hearts   8. Pass.
Even with such good support, the hand is too weak to give a raise.

(d)   1. Two spades 2. Two spades 3. Two spades 4. Two spades
5. Two spades   6. Four spades. A practical shot.   7. One no-trump.
Too weak for two clubs.   8. Pass.

29   **Exercise A :**   1. One no-trump. With a 4-3-3-3 pattern, prefer
1NT to raising the club suit.   2. One diamond. Change suit rather
than respond 1NT.   3. One heart. The major suit *opening* shows
five; responder's suits normally promise *four* or more.   4. One spade
5. One diamond. 4-card suits go up-the-line, even with the diamonds.
6. One heart.   7. One spade. Show the major rather than raise a
minor.   8. One diamond   9. One spade. Higher-ranking suit first
when holding a 5-5 pattern.   10. One spade. Show the major before
raising a minor.   11. One diamond. Up-the-line.   12. One heart.
Show the major, up-the-line, before raising a minor.   13. One spade
14. Two clubs. Raise a minor rather than show the other minor.
15. Two clubs   16. One diamond. Longest suit first.

Exercise B :   1. One spade. Up-the-line means "cheapest suit
first". One spade is cheaper than two clubs.   2. One spade. Any suit
quality is acceptable for a 4-card suit.   3. One no-trump. Too weak
for two clubs.   4. One no-trump. Too weak for two clubs. The

for two clubs. 4. One no-trump. Too weak for two clubs. The 1NT response may include a singleton (or even a void). Bidding two clubs with insufficient points is more dangerous. 5. Two hearts. The single raise with 3-card support is normal when playing 5-card majors. 6. Two hearts 7. Two hearts. Raise the major rather than show the other major. 8. Two hearts. Three points for the singleton makes this quite strong enough to raise to the two-level.

35   9. 1 club : 1 diamond, 1 spade : 1NT, Pass   10. 1 club : 1 heart, 2NT : 3 hearts, 4 hearts : Pass   11. Pass : 1 club, 2 clubs : 3NT, Pass 12. 1 club : 1 diamond, 1 heart : 2 hearts, Pass   13. Pass : 1 club, 1 spade : 4 spades, Pass   14. 1 spade : 1NT, 3 hearts : 4 hearts, Pass 15. Pass : 1 heart, 2 hearts : 3 hearts, 4 hearts : Pass   16. 1 spade : 1NT, 2NT : 3NT, Pass   17. Pass : 1 diamond, 1NT : Pass 18. 1 diamond : 1 heart, 1 spade : 2 diamonds, Pass   19. Pass : 1 club, 1 heart : 1 spade, 2 spades : Pass   20. 1 club : 1 heart, 1 spade : 2 spades, 4 spades : Pass.

41   **A.**   1. 2NT   2. 3NT   3. 1 diamond. No spade stopper makes 2NT unattractive.   4. 1 heart. Prefer a major suit reply to a reply in no-trumps.   5. 1 diamond. 4-card suits up-the-line.   6. 1 heart 7. 1 diamond   8. 1 heart. No need to rush with a strong hand.
B.   1. 3 diamonds   2. 1 heart   3. 1 heart   4. 1 spade
C.   1. 3 hearts   2. 1 spade. Do not give a jump raise with only three trumps   3. 2 clubs. 4-card suits up-the-line   4. 2 diamonds
D.   1. 2 diamonds   2. 2 hearts   3. 2 diamonds   4. 2 diamonds. Too strong for 2 spades and not strong enough for three spades. With such 10-12 point hands, change suit first and support later.
E.   1. 3 spades   2. 3 no-trumps   3. 4 hearts   4. 3 hearts

43   **A.**   1. 3 no-trumps   2. 3 hearts   3. 3 clubs   4. 3 no-trumps
B.   1. 2 no-trumps. Shows a minimum balanced hand after opening 1 diamond.   2. 3 no-trumps   3. 2 diamonds   4. 3 clubs
C.   1. 2 diamonds   2. 2 hearts. Not strong enough to bid 2 spades. A new suit rebid above 2 of the opened suit shows a strong opening, usually 16 points or more.   3. 2 hearts   4. 2 hearts.
D.   1. 3 spades   2. 4 hearts   3. 3 no-trumps   4. 3 diamonds
E.   1. 2 hearts   2. 2 spades. Not strong enough for 3 clubs, a new suit beyond 2 of the suit opened.   3. 3 spades   4. 4 spades

44   21. 1 club : 1 diamond, 1 spade : 3NT, Pass   22. 1 club : 1 diamond, 1 spade : 3NT, 4 spades : 5 clubs, Pass   23. 1 club : 1 heart, 3 clubs : 3 diamonds, 3NT   24. 1 club : 1 heart, 2 clubs : 2 diamonds, 2 hearts : 4 hearts, Pass   25. 1 club : 1 diamond, 1 heart : 1 spade,

2 spades: 4 spades, Pass   26. 1 club: 1 diamond, 1 heart: 3 diamonds,
3NT : Pass   27. 1 diamond : 2 clubs, 2NT : Pass
28. 1 diamond : 1 heart, 2 clubs : 3 clubs, 3NT : Pass
29. 1 diamond: 2 clubs, 2 diamonds: 2 hearts, 3 hearts: 4 hearts, Pass
30. 1 diamond : 1 heart, 2 clubs : 3 hearts, 4 hearts : Pass
31. 1 diamond : 1 heart, 2 diamonds : 3NT, Pass
32. 1 diamond : 1 spade, 2 clubs : 2 hearts, 3 clubs : 3NT, Pass

45   33. 1 heart : 1 spade, 2 hearts : 3 clubs, 3 spades : 4 spades, Pass
34. 1 heart: 1 spade, 2 hearts: 3 clubs, 3NT: Pass   35. 1 heart: 2 clubs,
2 diamonds: 2NT, 3NT: Pass   36. 1 heart: 2 clubs, 2 spades: 3 clubs,
3NT : Pass   37. 1 heart : 1 spade, 2 spades : 4 spades, Pass
38. 1 heart : 2 diamonds, 3 diamonds : 3 hearts, 4 hearts : Pass
39. 1 spade : 2 diamonds, 2 hearts : 2 spades, 4 spades : Pass
40. 1 spade : 2 diamonds, 2 hearts : 2NT, 3 hearts : 4 hearts, Pass
41. 1 spade : 2 diamonds, 2 hearts : 2NT, 3NT : Pass
42. 1 spade : 2 hearts, 3 diamonds : 3 hearts, 4 hearts : Pass
43. 1 spade : 2 hearts, 2 spades : Pass
44. 1 spade : 2 hearts, 3 hearts : 4 hearts, Pass

49   **A.**   1. 2 no-trumps   2. 1 heart   3. 2 spades   4. 3 clubs
B.   1. 3 hearts   2. 2 hearts   3. 2 no-trumps   4. 2 spades
5. 1 spade   6. 2 diamonds   7. 1 no-trump   8. 3 hearts
Partnership Bidding: 45. Pass: 1 heart, 3 hearts: 4 hearts, Pass
46. Pass : 1 club, 1 heart : 1 spade, 3 spades, 4 spades : Pass
47. Pass: 1 spade, 2 diamonds: Pass   48. Pass: 1 club, 1 spade: Pass
49. Pass: 1 club, 3 clubs: 3NT, Pass   50. Pass: 1 spade, 2 clubs: Pass

52   **A.**   1. 2 hearts   2. 2 diamonds   3. 2 hearts   4. 1 spade. Not enough
for a 2-opening   5. 2 hearts   6. 2 clubs
B.   1. 2 no-trumps   2. 2 no-trumps   3. 3 no-trumps   4. 3 diamonds
5. 3 hearts   6. 3 hearts   7. 4 hearts. Weaker than 3 hearts. 8. 2 spades
C.   1. 3 hearts   2. 4 spades   3. 3 spades   4. 3 no-trumps
5. 6 hearts. This shows you have 12 tricks in your own hand and asks
partner to choose between hearts and spades. Partner may revert
to 6 spades and should bid seven if holding the spade king   6. 3 clubs

53   **D.**   1. 3 no-trumps   2. 4 spades. Weaker than 3 spades.   3. 3 spades
4. 4 diamonds   5. 4 hearts   6. 4 spades   7. 3 no-trumps   8. 5 hearts
E.   1. 6 hearts   2. Pass   3. 6 hearts   4. 7 hearts
51. 2 diamonds: 2NT, 3 spades: 3NT   52. Pass: 2 clubs, 2NT: 3 spades,
3NT: 4 spades, Pass   53. 2 spades: 2NT, 3 spades: 4 spades, Pass
54. 2 diamonds: 2NT, 3 diamonds: 3 spades, 3NT   55. Pass: 2 spades,
2NT : 3 hearts, 4 hearts : Pass   56. Pass : 2NT, 3NT : Pass

60   **A.** 1. Slam zone. Bid 3 spades for now. Even if partner cannot
support spades, you are still strong enough for 6NT.   2. Slam zone.
Bid 3 diamonds for now. 3. Game zone. Bid 3NT. 14 points plus 16-18
does not add up to 33 points.   4. Game zone. Pass. 4 hearts is a weak,
shut-out raise.   5. Game zone. Bid 4 hearts. Partner may still bid on
with a powerful hand.   6. Slam zone. Partner's jump shows six hearts
and 16 points or more. Bid 4NT, asking for aces.
B. 1. 5 spades, showing three aces   2. 5 clubs, showing none or
four aces   3. 5 hearts. Two aces are missing.   4. 5 diamonds,
showing one ace   5. Pass. Five hearts was a sign-off. The 4NT asker
is in charge of how high to bid. Five hearts implies two aces are
missing.   6. 6 hearts, showing two kings.

61   **C.   a.** 6 spades. With one ace missing, bid the small slam. Do not
stop in 5 spades.   **b.** 6 spades. One king is missing and you cannot
tell which one it is.   **c.** 7NT. Partner has shown spade support,
two aces and two kings. That gives you thirteen tricks easily.
D.   a. Pass. The 4NT bidder is in control of the slam decisions.
Partner needs no support from you. Partner's diamonds will be
self-sufficient.   **b.** 6 spades. Here partner has bid two suits, spades
first and diamonds later. Partner is asking you to choose the trump
suit. You clearly prefer the spades.   **c.** 6 spades. This is the rare
exception when you may overrule partner's intended sign-off. You
have undisclosed support and an outside void.
E.   a. 5 no-trumps. Partner is attempting to sign off in no-trumps.
Partner cannot bid 5NT as this asks for kings. Bidding an unbid suit
at the 5-level asks partner to bid 5NT which can then be passed.
Apparently two aces are missing.   **b.** Pass. The raise to five in a
major asks partner to bid six with strong trumps. Your trumps are
no better than expected for a 1 spade opening.   **c.** 6 hearts. You
have strong hearts and that is what partner is asking of you.
Partnership Bidding: 57. 2 spades : 3 clubs, 3 hearts : 4 no-trumps,
5 spades : 6 no-trumps, Pass   58. 1 no-trump : 6 no-trumps, Pass
59. Pass : 2 hearts, 3 hearts : 4 no-trumps, 5 diamonds : 5 no-trumps,
6 hearts : 7 no-trumps. On finding an ace and two kings, East can
count 13 tricks.   60. 1 spade : 2 no-trumps, 3 hearts : 4 hearts,
4 no-trumps : 5 hearts, 5 no-trumps : 6 diamonds, 6 hearts : Pass
61. 2 no-trumps : 7 no-trumps. With no-trump hands, it is just a
matter of adding the points together.   62. 2 hearts : 2 no-trumps,
3 diamonds : 3 hearts, 4 no-trumps : 5 clubs, 5 no-trumps : 6 hearts,
7 no-trumps : Pass. Opposite two kings, West can count 13 tricks.

66 **A.** 1. Eight 2. Seven 3. Six 4. Seven and a half 5. Six and a half
6. Six 7. Six 8. Six 9. Four 10. Five 11. Six 12. Seven
13. Six 14. Five 15. Five 16. Six 17. Four 18. Six
B. (i) 1. 4 spades 2. 4 hearts 3. 1 club. Too strong for a pre-empt.
4. Five diamonds 5. 4 spades. Expectancy is eight playing tricks.
6. 3 clubs. A pre-empt with only a 6-card suit is rare but if the suit is
strong and you have the right number of playing tricks, it is all right.
7. Pass 8. Pass. Do not pre-empt with a 4-card major on the side.
9. Pass. The spades are too weak. Only five playing tricks potential.
10. Pass. If you must bid, open 1 spade. 11. One heart. Too strong
for a pre-empt. 12. 4 hearts. The typical pre-empt has a long, strong
suit and little else. 13. Pass. Only five playing tricks potential.
14. 2 spades. Do not pre-empt when you have a powerful hand.
15. 4 spades. It is all right to have a minor suit on the side.
(ii) 1. 3 spades. Seven playing tricks. When vulnerable, add two to
your playing trick potential. 2. 3 hearts 3. 1 club 4. 5 diamonds
5. 4 spades 6. Pass 7. Pass 8. Pass 9. Pass 10. Pass 11. 1 heart
12. 3 hearts 13. Pass 14. 2 spades 15. 4 spades. Optimistic,
perhaps, but there are six playing tricks in spades and there could
be two in the clubs.

67 **C.** (i) 1. Pass 2. Pass 3. Pass. Do not "rescue" partner on a
misfit with a weak hand. 4. 3 spades. Partner should support with
a doubleton or better. 5. Pass. You need more than three winners
to raise a non-vulnerable pre-empt. 6. 4 hearts. Three winners
plus potential for a fourth trick via a spade ruff. 7. 3 no-trumps.
With a double stopper in every suit outside partner's, this is a sound
risk with a balanced hand. 8. 4 hearts. With nine hearts between
you, spades is unlikely to be a better trump fit. 9. 4 hearts 10. Pass
11. 4 no-trumps. If partner has the ace of hearts, you should bid 7NT.
12. 4 no-trumps. If partner has an ace, bid 6 hearts.
(ii) 1. Pass 2. Pass 3. Pass 4. 3 spades 5. 4 hearts. To raise a
vulnerable pre-empt, more than two winners is enough. 6. 4 hearts
7. 3 no-trumps 8. 4 hearts 9. 4 hearts 10. Pass 11. 4 no-trumps
12. 4 no-trumps
Bidding: 63. 3 spades: 4 spades, Pass. 64. 3 diamonds: 3NT, Pass
65. 3 diamonds: 3 spades, 4 spades: Pass 66. Pass: 3 hearts, Pass
67. 4 spades: 4NT, 5 diamonds: 6 spades, Pass 68. 3 diamonds: 3 hearts,
4 hearts: 4NT, 5 diamonds: 6 hearts, Pass. Change of suit is forcing
after a pre-empt. Once East receives heart support, slam should be
bid if West shows an ace.

73   **A.**   1. Pass   2. Bid 1NT   3. Double. With the strength for a 1NT
overcall but no stopper in their suit, force partner to reply by doubling
and judge the best next move after partner's reply.   4. Pass. With
length and strength in the enemy suit, the best strategy is usually to
pass and defend.
B.   1. 1 spade   2. 1 spade   3. Pass   4. 1 diamond   5. Pass   6. 4 spades
7. 1 spade. With a 5-5 pattern, start with the higher-ranking suit.
8. 2 hearts. Strong jump overcall.   9. Pass. Suit too weak to overcall.
C.   1. 2 diamonds   2. Pass. Suit too weak to overcall.   3. 3 clubs.
Strong jump overcall. You hope partner can bid 3NT.   4. 3 no-trumps.
You figure to take nine tricks on a spade lead. 3NT is a good gamble.
5. 2 hearts   6. Pass   7. 5 diamonds. Pre-emptive. Worth the risk.
8. 2 diamonds   9. Pass. The clubs do not meet the Suit Quality
Test for 2 clubs and the spade length is a drawback to an overcall.

74   **D.**   1. Pass   2. 1 spade   3. 4 spades. Bid up on the freak hands.
E.   1. Pass. If the opponents' bidding is genuine, partner can have
scarcely one point.   2. 4 hearts. A reasonable shot.   3. Pass. As
with the first hand, partner can have very little. Your hand is good
for defending, not for playing with only 5-6 tricks potential.
F.   1. Pass   2. 4 hearts   3. 2 hearts   4. 3 hearts   5. 2 diamonds
6. 1 no-trump   7. 2 no-trumps   8. 1 spade   9. 3 no-trumps
G.   1. 3 spades   2. 4 spades   3. 2 no-trumps

75   **Bidding :**   69. (1 club) : 1 heart : 1 no-trump, 2 hearts : Pass
70. (1 club) : 1 no-trump : 4 hearts, Pass   71. (1 diamond) : 2 hearts :
4 hearts, Pass   72. (1 diamond) : 1 heart : 3 hearts, 4 hearts : Pass
73. (1 heart) : 1 no-trump : 2 no-trumps, 3 no-trumps : Pass
74. (1 heart) : 2 spades : 4 spades, Pass   75. (1 heart) : 2 diamonds :
2 spades, 3 spades : 4 spades, Pass   76. (1 spade) : 2 clubs : 2 no-trumps,
3 no-trumps : Pass   77. (1 spade) : Pass : 3 hearts, 4 hearts : Pass
78. (1 spade) : 2 clubs : 3 no-trumps, Pass

81   **A.**   1. Takeout 2. Takeout 3. Takeout 4. Penalties 5. Penalties.
Double of a 1NT opening is for penalties.   6. Penalties. Double
after a 1NT opening is for penalties.
B.   1. Double   2. Double   3. 1 diamond. Lack of support for
hearts makes this unattractive for a double   4. Double. If partner
bids diamonds, you can bid hearts.   5. Double. With only four losers,
the hand is too powerful for even a strong jump-overcall.   6. 1 spade.
Lack of heart support makes a double unappealing.   7. Double.
8. 1 no-trump. If the hand fits a 1NT overcall, prefer that bid.
9. Double. Double-and-no-trumps-later is stronger than 1NT at once.

C. 1. Pass 2. Pass. With 12-15 hcp, if your hand is not suitable for an overcall or a takeout double, pass. You are expected to open with 13 points but you need not take action with an unsuitable 13 point hand after the opposition have opened. 3. Double. The right ingredients for a takeout double with minimum point count are shortage in the enemy suit and 3-4 cards in each of the other suits. 4. 1 spade. Prefer to show a strong 5-card or longer holding in the other major by bidding the major. 5. Double. With only four cards in the other major, double works better and is superior to bidding the diamonds. 6. Pass. The more you have in their suit, the better it is to defend. 7. 1 no-trump. If the conditions are right, prefer the 1 no-trump to a double. 8. Double. Too strong for 1 no-trump. 9. Double. Too big for even a strong jump-overcall.

82 **D.** 1. 1 spade 2. 1 spade. This hand makes Hand 1 look great. 3. 1 spade 4. 1 heart. Choose a major rather than a minor in response to a double even when the major is shorter or weaker. 5. 2 clubs 6. 1 heart. With no 4-card suit to bid (you would not want to bid their suit), choose your cheapest 3-card suit.
E. 1. 2 spades. Too strong for 1 spade. Worth 10 points if you count your singleton. 2. 2 hearts. Too big for 1 heart. Count your doubletons and you have 10 points. 3. 2 diamonds. Not 1 diamond. 4. 1 no-trump 5. 2 no-trumps 6. 4 spades. A sound approach when answering a takeout double is to imagine partner has opened in your best suit. If partner had opened 1 spade, you would not settle for less than game.
F. 1. Pass. You are no longer obliged to bid. 2. 2 hearts. However, you are not forced to pass. Over an intervening bid, you should bid with 6 points or more. Again, imagine partner had opened 1 heart. You would not hesitate then to bid 2 hearts over a 1 spade overcall. 3. 3 hearts. If you are worth a jump, make the jump reply over the intervention. Had South passed, you would have jumped to 2 hearts.
G. 1. Pass. 2. 2 hearts 3. 3 hearts. Partner may have no points.

83 **Partnership Bidding:** 79. (1 heart) : Double : 2 diamonds, Pass
80. (1 heart) : Double : 2 clubs, Pass 81. (1 club) : Double : 1 spade, 2 spades : Pass 82. (1 club) : Double : 1 heart, 3 hearts : Pass
83. (1 diamond) : Double : 1 spade, Pass 84. (1 heart) : Double : 1 no-trump, 2 no-trumps : 3 no-trumps, Pass. 85. (1 spade) : Double : 2 no-trumps, 3 no-trumps : Pass 86. (1 heart) : Double : 2 spades, Pass
87. (1 club) : Double, 4 spades : Pass
88. (1 diamond) : Double : 3 clubs, 3 hearts : 4 hearts, Pass

Play Hands for NORTH (* = dealer)

1*	2	3	4	5*	6
♠ AQJ7	♠ Q1092	♠ 7543	♠ J92	♠ AQ53	♠ K10974
♥ 943	♥ 32	♥ QJ109	♥ AK2	♥ 863	♥ 10
◇ Q75	◇ J6	◇ KJ10	◇ KQJ	◇ 742	◇ 1052
♣ 642	♣ 98754	♣ 106	♣ 8632	♣ 1085	♣ 10843

7	8	9*	10	11	12
♠ Q98	♠ 874	♠ AKQ983	♠ 106	♠ 53	♠ 54
♥ 7654	♥ Q96	♥ A86	♥ 82	♥ 92	♥ 86
◇ AQ	◇ Q8	◇ Q3	◇ 9843	◇ KQ93	◇ A10932
♣ AKQJ	♣ KJ942	♣ J10	♣ K10642	♣ J8742	♣ 10754

13*	14	15	16	17*	18
♠ 1074	♠ - - -	♠ A975	♠ - - -	♠ AQJ3	♠ 10
♥ AKQ10	♥ 10854	♥ KQ42	♥ 109632	♥ AK	♥ J109532
◇ K	◇ A753	◇ 852	◇ 97542	◇ AJ42	◇ 98
♣ J8762	♣ 87432	♣ KQ	♣ AK8	♣ QJ9	♣ A872

19	20	21*	22	23	24
♠ A	♠ 8	♠ 9652	♠ J6	♠ AKQJ2	♠ Q109
♥ 86532	♥ QJ974	♥ J10943	♥ 97532	♥ KQJ4	♥ J1098
◇ 7432	◇ Q10742	◇ 652	◇ A2	◇ AQJ	◇ Q109
♣ 753	♣ 92	♣ 10	♣ AQJ5	♣ 2	♣ 965

25*	26	27	28	29*	30
♠ AKQ9765	♠ KQ76	♠ J	♠ 106432	♠ AK	♠ 65
♥ 2	♥ K10873	♥ AQJ	♥ - - -	♥ K862	♥ 2
◇ 8	◇ J98	◇ K109	◇ K932	◇ KQ1093	◇ J7643
♣ 9873	♣ 2	♣ A98763	♣ 10876	♣ 105	♣ J7542

31	32	33*	34	35	36
♠ 52	♠ AK	♠ J108743	♠ 8	♠ AKQJ	♠ KQJ107
♥ A932	♥ A109852	♥ 6	♥ KJ10654	♥ K753	♥ K862
◇ 82	◇ K3	◇ 1095	◇ A6	◇ K	◇ 94
♣ J9864	♣ KJ10	♣ J53	♣ J962	♣ Q432	♣ A10

Play Hands for EAST (* = dealer)

1	2*	3	4	5	6*
♠ 109432	♠ AJ3	♠ AK102	♠ 108753	♠ 10982	♠ 853
♡ 5	♡ Q54	♡ A4	♡ Q76	♡ Q54	♡ A432
◇ J1096	◇ AK52	◇ 643	◇ 972	◇ KQJ9	◇ AKQJ
♣ KQ10	♣ 1063	♣ 8532	♣ K9	♣ K2	♣ Q5

7	8	9	10*	11	12
♠ KJ3	♠ Q1032	♠ J	♠ AQ43	♠ 7642	♠ 732
♡ KQJ9	♡ 854	♡ KQJ1053	♡ AK7	♡ 107	♡ QJ1095
◇ 8752	◇ 963	◇ A982	◇ KQ1072	◇ AJ108	◇ K76
♣ 106	♣ A65	♣ 93	♣ 9	♣ A109	♣ 62

13	14*	15	16	17	18*
♠ 952	♠ 976432	♠ 108632	♠ K52	♠ 754	♠ 8643
♡ - - -	♡ AKQ	♡ J865	♡ QJ7	♡ 9542	♡ 87
◇ 1087654	◇ Q9	◇ 94	◇ AKQ	◇ KQ109	◇ 5432
♣ 10543	♣ Q9	♣ 75	♣ J942	♣ 103	♣ 543

19	20	21	22*	23	24
♠ 9742	♠ AKQ5432	♠ AK7	♠ KQ10	♠ 96543	♠ AJ73
♡ K107	♡ AK	♡ A82	♡ QJ8	♡ A8	♡ KQ
◇ 965	◇ AJ	◇ AQ3	◇ 84	◇ K2	◇ 873
♣ AKQ	♣ J8	♣ KQ54	♣ K9762	♣ 9654	♣ QJ104

25	26*	27	28	29	30*
♠ 10	♠ 42	♠ AQ762	♠ A95	♠ 6543	♠ Q842
♡ KQJ83	♡ Q4	♡ K5432	♡ K1054	♡ 95	♡ QJ107
◇ AJ5	◇ 63	◇ 7	◇ A6	◇ A	◇ Q98
♣ 6542	♣ KQJ8763	♣ 102	♣ AKQJ	♣ AQJ863	♣ K9

31	32	33	34*	35	36
♠ AKJ984	♠ Q6	♠ A2	♠ J543	♠ 109742	♠ 5
♡ K	♡ J	♡ 98732	♡ AQ2	♡ 1086	♡ AQJ10
◇ K75	◇ QJ10964	◇ K3	◇ KQJ84	◇ A103	◇ AQ52
♣ 1053	♣ AQ87	♣ Q1062	♣ Q	♣ 95	♣ K872

Play Hands for SOUTH (* = dealer)

1	2	3*	4	5	6
♠ K8	♠ K54	♠ 986	♠ KQ	♠ KJ4	♠ A6
♡ A76	♡ AJ10987	♡ K875	♡ J43	♡ AK72	♡ KQJ97
◇ K432	◇ Q1087	◇ A97	◇ A10653	◇ A85	◇ 983
♣ A973	♣ - - -	♣ 974	♣ QJ4	♣ J63	♣ 972

7*	8	9	10	11*	12
♠ 764	♠ 965	♠ 7654	♠ 752	♠ AK9	♠ KQJ106
♡ A8	♡ KJ102	♡ 972	♡ QJ1093	♡ AK8643	♡ A73
◇ KJ104	◇ KJ107	◇ J54	◇ A6	◇ 76	◇ 54
♣ 8432	♣ Q3	♣ AKQ	♣ AQ5	♣ Q5	♣ J98

13	14	15*	16	17	18
♠ QJ	♠ Q108	♠ K	♠ Q986	♠ 862	♠ QJ9
♡ 76543	♡ 96	♡ A1073	♡ A5	♡ QJ8763	♡ A64
◇ QJ32	◇ 10862	◇ J63	◇ 863	◇ 7	◇ Q107
♣ AK	♣ AK105	♣ AJ1093	♣ Q1075	♣ 865	♣ J1096

19*	20	21	22	23*	24
♠ KQ86	♠ J109	♠ 1083	♠ A2	♠ 7	♠ - - -
♡ AQJ	♡ 86	♡ 75	♡ AK64	♡ 1097532	♡ 765432
◇ AKQ	◇ K5	◇ J1098	◇ KQJ765	◇ 63	◇ J62
♣ J42	♣ AK6543	♣ A976	♣ 8	♣ AKJ3	♣ A732

25	26	27*	28	29	30
♠ 42	♠ J85	♠ 8	♠ KQJ8	♠ QJ72	♠ A7
♡ A7	♡ J92	♡ 107	♡ QJ	♡ AQJ107	♡ A86543
◇ 976432	◇ Q7542	◇ AQJ865432	◇ 8754	◇ J4	◇ AK
♣ QJ10	♣ A10	♣ 5	♣ 952	♣ 94	♣ 1063

31*	32	33	34	35*	36
♠ 76	♠ J109	♠ 9	♠ AK106	♠ 63	♠ 864
♡ QJ1076	♡ KQ63	♡ AJ10	♡ 983	♡ AJ42	♡ 95
◇ AQ63	◇ 82	◇ Q872	◇ 52	◇ 9864	◇ 10763
♣ A2	♣ 6532	♣ AK987	♣ AK74	♣ 1076	♣ 9643

Play Hands for WEST (* = dealer)

1	2	3	4*	5	6
♠ 65	♠ 876	♠ QJ	♠ A64	♠ 76	♠ QJ2
♡ KQJ1082	♡ K6	♡ 632	♡ 10985	♡ J109	♡ 865
◇ A8	◇ 943	◇ Q852	◇ 84	◇ 1063	◇ 764
♣ J85	♣ AKQJ2	♣ AKQJ	♣ A1075	♣ AQ974	♣ AKJ6

7	8*	9	10	11	12*
♠ A1052	♠ AKJ	♠ 102	♠ KJ98	♠ QJ108	♠ A98
♡ 1032	♡ A73	♡ 4	♡ 654	♡ QJ5	♡ K42
◇ 963	◇ A542	◇ K1076	◇ J5	◇ 542	◇ QJ8
♣ 975	♣ 1087	♣ 876542	♣ J873	♣ K63	♣ AKQ3

13	14	15	16*	17	18
♠ AK863	♠ AKJ5	♠ QJ4	♠ AJ10743	♠ K109	♠ AK752
♡ J982	♡ J732	♡ 9	♡ K84	♡ 10	♡ KQ
◇ A9	◇ KJ4	◇ AKQ107	◇ J10	◇ 8653	◇ AKJ6
♣ Q9	♣ J6	♣ 8642	♣ 63	♣ AK742	♣ KQ

19	20*	21	22	23	24*
♠ J1053	♠ 76	♠ QJ4	♠ 987543	♠ 108	♠ K86542
♡ 94	♡ 10532	♡ KQ6	♡ 10	♡ 6	♡ A
◇ J108	◇ 9863	◇ K74	◇ 1093	◇ 1098754	◇ AK54
♣ 10986	♣ Q107	♣ J832	♣ 1043	♣ Q1087	♣ K8

25	26	27	28*	29	30
♠ J83	♠ A1093	♠ K109543	♠ 7	♠ 1098	♠ KJ1093
♡ 109654	♡ A65	♡ 986	♡ A987632	♡ 43	♡ K9
◇ KQ10	◇ AK10	◇ - - -	◇ QJ10	◇ 87652	◇ 1052
♣ AK	♣ 954	♣ KQJ4	♣ 43	♣ K72	♣ AQ8

31	32*	33	34	35	36*
♠ Q103	♠ 875432	♠ KQ65	♠ Q972	♠ 85	♠ A932
♡ 854	♡ 74	♡ KQ54	♡ 7	♡ Q9	♡ 743
◇ J1094	◇ A75	◇ AJ64	◇ 10973	◇ QJ752	◇ KJ8
♣ KQ7	♣ 94	♣ 4	♣ 10853	♣ AKJ8	♣ QJ5

WHAT DO RESPONDER'S BIDS MEAN?

Action	Meaning of Partner's Action	Page
1NT : 2♣	Stayman Convention, asking for opener's majors.	93
1NT : 2◇/2♡/2♠	Weakness rescue from 1NT. Opener should pass.	30
1NT : 2NT	Inviting game. Opener bids on if better than minimum.	22
1NT : 3-any-suit	Forcing to game. 5-card suit. Opener raises with 3.	39
1NT : 3NT	Sign-off in game. Opener must pass.	22
1NT : 4♡ or 4♠	Sign-off in game. 6-card or longer suit. Opener passes.	39
1♣ : 1◇/1♡/1♠	One-over-one response. 6 or more points. Forcing.	27, 38
1♣ : 2◇/2♡/2♠	Jump-shift. Game force. Suggests slam is likely.	38, 39
1♣ : 3◇/3♡/3♠	Pre-emptive response, very weak hand, 7-8-card suit.	64
1♣ : 4♡ or 4♠	Pre-emptive response, very weak hand, 8-card suit.	64
1♣/1◇ : 2♣/2◇	Weak. No major. Opener passes below 16 points.	26, 28
1♣/1◇ : 3♣/3◇	Strong raise but still denies a major suit.	38, 39
1♣/1◇ : 1NT	Weak response. Denies a major. Used as last resort.	27, 28
1♣/1◇ : 2NT	Strong balanced hand. Normally denies a major suit.	38, 39
1♣/1◇ : 3NT	Stronger balanced hand. Denies a major suit.	38, 39
1◇ : 1♡/1♠	4-card or longer suit, 6 or more points. Forcing.	27, 38
1◇ : 2♣	4-card or longer suit, 10 or more points. Forcing.	38, 39
1◇ : 2♡/2♠/3♣	Jump-shift. Game force. Suggests slam is likely.	38, 39
1◇ : 3♡/3♠	Pre-emptive response, very weak hand, 7-8-card suit	64
1◇ : 4♡/4♠	Pre-emptive response, very weak hand, 8-card suit.	64
1♡/1♠ : 2♡/2♠	Weak raise. Opener passes below 16 points.	26, 28
1♡/1♠ : 3♡/3♠	Strong raise.	38, 39
1♡/1♠ : 4♡/4♠	Pre-emptive raise. Normally 6-10 HCP, unbalanced.	30
1♡/1♠ : 1NT	Weak response. 1 ? : 1NT denies four spades.	27, 28
1♡/1♠ : 2NT	Strong balanced hand.	38, 39
1♡/1♠ : 3NT	Stronger balanced hand.	38, 39
1♡ : 1♠	Four or more spades, six or more points. Forcing.	27, 38
1♡/1♠ : 2♣/2◇	4-card or longer suit, 10 or more points. Forcing.	38, 39
1♠ : 2♡	*Five* or more hearts, 10 or more points. Forcing.	38, 40
1♡/1♠ : 3♣/3◇	Jump-shift. Game force. Suggests slam is likely.	38, 39
Any Suit : 4NT	Blackwood Convention, asking for aces.	58, 59
2NT : 3♣	Stayman (For Baron Convention, see page 106)	93
2NT : 3♡/3♠	5-card suit. Forcing to game. Opener raises with 3.	50
2NT : 4♡/4♠	Sign-off in game. 6-card or longer suit. Opener passes.	50